CENSORSHIP AND FIRST AMENDMENT RIGHTS: A PRIMER

PUBLISHED BY THE

AMERICAN BOOKSELLERS FOUNDATION FOR FREE EXPRESSION

Editor: Thelma Adams

Cover Design: Ira Cook

Book Design: Linda Miller

Typesetting: Christina Vlachos

Advisory Board: Daniel W. Chartrand, James L. Dana, Deborah D. Garman, Rhett Jackson, Lisa Knudsen, Max Lillienstein, Melissa J. Mytinger, Bernard E. Rath, Larry Robin, Chuck Robinson, Oren J. Teicher, Susan E. Walker

ISBN: 1-879556-05-7

American Booksellers Foundation for Free Expression
560 White Plains Road
Tarrytown, NY 10591

Contents

Preface

Exactly two hundred years ago, those few brief words we now know as the First Amendment became the law of the land. And we, as Americans, became one of the first societies in the history of civilization to set down in writing those precious guarantees that now so many of us take for granted.

The American Booksellers Foundation for Free Expression believes that we should not take the First Amendment for granted—and that is why we have prepared this book. Our hope is to inform those involved in the dissemination of words—and the reading public as well—that the freedom of speech is under attack every day, and unless we do something about it our rights will continue to erode.

As people involved in the bookselling community, we believe we have a special responsibility to ensure the availability of the widest range of reading material to the public—and deeply oppose any and all efforts to interfere with an individual's access to constitutionally protected material.

In early 1990, under the leadership of Joyce Meskis, the owner of the Tattered Cover in Denver, Colorado, the Board of Directors of the American Booksellers Association, in an effort to do more to oppose censorship and to support free expression, voted to fund the creation of a new organization whose goal was to "inform and educate booksellers, other members of the book industry and the public about the deleterious effects of censorship; to actively promote and protect the free expression of ideas, particularly freedom of choice of reading material." One of the early priorities of that new organization—which became known as the American Booksellers Foundation for Free Expression—was to prepare the book you now hold in your hand. It is our hope that the information that follows will be helpful in our joint efforts to ensure that there will be many more anniversaries of the First Amendment!

I have had the privilege over the past eighteen months to work with a remarkable group of people who have become the Board of Directors of this fledgling effort. I have come to know them not just as dedicated representatives of the bookselling community but as individuals who do more than just talk—they act! This book is the result of their work, and would never have existed without them. While several of their names appear in connection with individual chapters, this book is the work of the entire group: Dan Chartrand, Jim Dana, Debbie Garman, Rhett Jackson, Lisa Knudsen, Max Lillienstein, Melissa Mytinger, Bernie Rath, Larry Robin, Chuck Robinson, and Susan Walker. I thank each of them not just for what they have done to make this book possible, but for all they represent every day in supporting free expression and opposing censorship. I am genuinely honored to be associated with each of them.

I should also say that Joyce Meskis' leadership of the American Booksellers Association these several years has been indispensable in sharpening our role in the First Amendment area. Joyce Meskis puts her money where her mouth is every day of every year by never yielding to those who would compromise the First Amendment. She leads by example, and booksellers could not have been better served by her innumerable contributions to our efforts. She is the underlying reason why this Foundation—and this book—exist.

In addition, allow me to thank Thelma Adams, who has done a really fine job as our editor, and Linda Miller, the Publishing Director of the American Booksellers Association, whose quiet but always reliable advice contributed immeasurably to this effort.

Finally, I'd like to thank the thousands of booksellers from all across this country who make it their business to promote free expression in their stores by the vast array of reading matter they choose to make available to the public. Without them, the fight to protect the First Amendment would most assuredly be lost.

Oren J. Teicher
President
American Booksellers Foundation
for Free Expression

The Bill of Rights: The First 200 Years

BY ANTHONY LEWIS

I n December of this year we shall celebrate the bicentennial of the Bill of Rights, the first ten amendments to the Constitution. If I were to attempt to discuss all ten and what has happened to them over the last two centuries, I could go on for pages and pages and barely begin to touch the subject. So I shall narrow the focus to the provisions of the Bill of Rights that may be closest to the hearts of booksellers and certainly to journalists: the First Amendment's guarantees of free speech and press.

"Congress shall make no law abridging the freedom of speech or of the press." Those are the words. How simple they sound. We tend to take for granted that they assure us the remarkably open society we have, I think the freest in the world. We Americans can read books banned in England or Israel; we can denounce our leaders; we can even burn our flag without fear of punishment. But of course it is not so simple. When the First Amendment was ratified in 1791, its words did not establish our freedom. It has taken much history, a turbulent, embattled history, to give meaning to those words.

Anthony Lewis is a Pulitzer Prize winning columnist for the New York Times. *This essay was transcribed from an address Mr. Lewis delivered at the American Booksellers Association Convention in New York City on June 2, 1991.*

Just seven years after the Bill of Rights was ratified in 1798 the Federalist party that then controlled Congress pushed through a Sedition Act that made it a crime to publish false, scandalous and malicious comments about the President or either House of Congress. Note that the act punished nasty comments about the President, John Adams, a Federalist, but not about the Vice President, Thomas Jefferson, who was, in a sense, the leader of the opposition—the then just emerging party of Jeffersonians, Republicans, Democrats as they eventually became.

It was partisan legislation, openly so. The Federalists planned to silence the main Jeffersonian newspapers in the period leading up to the presidential election of the year 1800, and they tried. The editors and owners of those papers were all prosecuted. But the first case was brought against a member of the House of Representatives, Matthew Lyon of Vermont. He had written a letter to the editor of the Vermont Journal, saying that the chief executive, Adams, was engaged in "a continual grasp for power, in an unbounded thirst for ridiculous pomp, foolish adulation and selfish avarice." The indictment charged that his words were scurrilous, feigned, false, scandalous, seditious, and malicious. He was convicted and sentenced to four months in prison and a fine of $1000, an enormous sum in those days, and one that incidentally, he could not pay. He remained in prison until others raised the money. And all of that for words that would strike you as rather anodyne by today's standards.

When the Sedition Act was passed, Jefferson and James Madison decided to try to arouse opposition to it in state legislatures. They worked in secret for fear that they would be prosecuted themselves. The Vice President, I remind you, and a leading member of Congress. Madison wrote what came to be called the Virginia Resolutions, important documents in our freedom. "The Sedition Act," Madison said, "ought to produce universal alarm because it is leveled against the right of freely examining public characters and measures, and of free communication among the people thereon, which has ever been justly deemed the only effectual guardian of every other right."

Madison's words may sound a bit antique, but his thought is as vital today as ever—not only here but in Beijing and Moscow and Prague. The right to examine public characters and measures, in short to criticize government officials and their policies, is crucial to democracy. In punishing such criticism, Madison said, the Sedition Act violated the First Amendment. He went on to make a fundamental point about the nature of our political system: "In this country, the people, not the government, possess the absolute sovereignty." That was altogether different from Britain, where even today Parliament is sovereign, and where the kind of rights that we take for granted do not exist for the press, for publishers, for individuals.

If all of us, the people, the citizens, are the ultimate rulers, it follows that we must be able to examine and criticize those whom we choose to govern us from time to time. Not everyone agreed with the Madisonian view. John Marshall, later the great Chief Justice of the United States, was a Federalist candidate for Congress in 1798, and he supported the Sedition Act. Marshall wrote that the state must be able to protect itself "from the attempts of wicked citizens to disturb the public repose. Government cannot be secure if by falsehood and malicious slander it is to be deprived of the confidence and affection of the people." Marshall really articulated the premise underlying the Sedition Act: Government is a fragile creature that must be protected from wicked citizens. It is a very English view.

If that view had prevailed in the United States, it would be a much more decorous country. We would not have the open society that is the distinctive feature of America. The constitutionality of the Sedition Act was never tested in the Supreme Court. But as a political tactic it proved to be a disaster. It aroused popular outrage and helped the Jeffersonians in the election of 1800. Large numbers of Americans became aware of what I call the Madisonian premise, the role of free speech in a democracy. Jefferson defeated Adams. On taking office he pardoned all those who had been convicted under the Sedition Act. A few years later he explained why in a letter to John Adams's wife, Abigail. "I considered that law to be a nullity," he said [that is, unconstitutional], "as absolute and palpable as if Congress had ordered us to fall down and worship a golden image." Isn't it wonderful, by the way, that despite their bitter political differences, they corresponded? Jefferson and John Adams remained friendly correspondents until the day they both died, July 4th, 1826, the fiftieth anniversary of the Declaration of Independence.

I have taken you a long way back in history, for a reason. That was the first test of the theory of the First Amendment, which I think is the theory of our Constitution. And it was more than one hundred years before there was another test of any significance, more than a century until Congress again passed legislation that had the effect of punishing political speech.

In 1917, when the United States entered World War I, the mood of the country turned violently jingoistic. Sauerkraut was called "liberty cabbage." Dissent from the war was not tolerated. In that atmosphere Congress passed an Espionage Act that among other things made it a crime to cause or attempt to cause insubordination or disloyalty in the military or naval forces or to obstruct the recruiting or enlistment service. The latter clause was invoked in 1918 against Eugene V. Debs, a socialist and pacifist who was five times the Socialist party's candidate for president. By common consent today he is considered an outstanding figure of his day.

Debs made a speech in Canton, Ohio, mostly about socialism. But he also said he had just visited three colleagues who were in jail for aiding someone in failing to register for the draft and that, "they were paying the penalty for seeking to pave the way to better conditions for all mankind." He was prosecuted for those words, convicted and sentenced to ten years in prison. He took the case to the Supreme Court, arguing that the conviction violated his right to free speech under the First Amendment. But the Court unanimously rejected the claim and upheld the conviction in an opinion by Justice Holmes.

Think about that case, the Debs case, in comparison with what we have seen and heard in our own lifetimes by way of antiwar statements. Thousands of Americans, I suppose hundreds of thousands, made far harsher statements against the Vietnam War than Eugene Debs did in World War I. Stronger words were used against American participation in the Persian Gulf War, but no one went to prison for mere words during Vietnam, nor, I dare say, will any dissenters from the Gulf War.

What has happened to the law, to the received meaning of the First Amendment? In fact, there has been an extraordinary historical process, beginning just a few months after the Debs decision. Another Espionage Act case was decided by the Supreme Court, this one involving three anarchists and a socialist who protested President Wilson's dispatch of American troops to intervene in Russia after the Bolshevik Revolution. The Court again upheld the convictions, which were for protesting, in some small leaflets thrown from the roof of a building in the New York garment district, the policy of sending troops to what was becoming the Soviet Union. But this time Justice Holmes dissented.

His opinion read in part:

> Persecution for the expression of opinions seems to me perfectly logical. If you have no doubt of your premises or your power and you want a certain result with all your heart, you naturally express your wishes in law and sweep away all opposition.... But when men have come to realize that time has upset many fighting faiths, they may come to believe even more than the foundations of their own conduct that the ultimate good desired is better reached by free trade in ideas—that the best test of truth is the power of the thought to get itself accepted in the competition of the market.... That at any rate is the theory of our Constitution. It is an experiment, as all life is an

> experiment.... While that experiment is part of our system, I think that we should be eternally vigilant against attempts to check the expression of opinions that we loathe and believe to be fraught with death....

I thought to myself some time ago, after quite a long time in the business of writing, that I would be glad to have written one sentence as good as, "It is an experiment, as all life is an experiment." That dissenting opinion was the beginning of the Supreme Court's recognition of freedom of expression as a paramount constitutional value.

Holmes was joined in that dissent, and then in others, by Justice Brandeis. In 1927 Brandeis wrote a dissenting opinion, joined by Holmes, that I think was an even greater statement of the reasoning behind the case for freedom of speech. Brandeis said:

> Those who won our independence ... believed liberty to be the secret of happiness and courage to be the secret of liberty. They believed that freedom to think as you will and to speak as you think are means indispensable to the discovery of political truth; ... that the greatest menace to freedom is an inert people, that public discussion is a political duty.... Fear of serious injury alone cannot justify suppression of free speech and assembly. Men feared witches and burnt women. It is the function of speech to free men from the bondage of irrational fears.

The theme of that astonishing passage is civic courage. Brandeis's repeated rejection of fear as a ground for repression gave some of us courage in the dark times that came over this country after World War II. The image of witch-burning was not far from reality in the period when Senator Joe McCarthy won headlines by accusing people of treason. And when many politicians vied to see who could invent the most vindictive and the most pointless legislation against Communism.

If the words of Holmes and Brandeis were no more than ringing protests against the intolerance of their day, I suppose they might be remembered mostly for their literary value. But they were much more. Gradually, over the years, those dissents became the law of the First Amendment. The Holmes–

Brandeis view persuaded the country and, in time, persuaded the Supreme Court. That tells us something about the remarkable nature of the Court as an institution of government.

The Framers of our Constitution expected the Court to be weak. It had "neither sword nor purse," Alexander Hamilton said. It had only the power to persuade. But that has proved enough to defeat presidents and Congresses, enough to give the Supreme Court the last word in much of American life. To have that role, the Court must convince us that it speaks for values more permanent than a passing majority's wishes, values that underlie our existence as a nation. Holmes and Brandeis had only two votes of nine. Their power was in their rhetoric. They taught the country and the Court that freedom of speech was a fundamental value, essential to our constitutional system.

I repeat, we take that for granted. It could not be taken for granted before the Holmes and Brandeis dissents.

History came full cycle in 1964. The case was called *New York Times* v. *Sullivan*. What is relevant here is that Justice Brennan, writing the opinion of the Court, considered the history of the Sedition Act of 1798 at length. He quoted Madison's words about how the act had interfered with the right to examine public characters and measures, and he agreed. Justice Brennan concluded, "Although the Sedition Act was never tested in this Court, the attack upon its validity has carried the day in the court of history." With that, the statute that expired in 1801 was retrospectively, 163 years later, held unconstitutional.

Have we been true to the bold promise of the First Amendment and of the judges who have made it meaningful in our time? The history I have so episodically sketched suggests that now the answer is, yes. Gradually, over time, we have come to understand the importance of free speech as Madison understood it. The decisions from which Holmes and Brandeis dissented have been overruled by the Supreme Court. The First Amendment today gives all of us a broad assurance that we can think what we want and say what we think without fear of punishment.

But history is not an ascending curve. There have been dark passages in the record of the First Amendment. In the Palmer Raids of 1920, federal agents arrested 4,000 supposed radicals around the country in a single night. Fear of Communism led to other repressive excesses over many years. Not just Joe McCarthy, but other committees of the House and Senate intimidated all kinds of people for their political views, imposing black lists in Hollywood and local government security checks on teachers and other employees. And I have to tell you that the Supreme Court did very little to hold those outrages up to the test of the First Amendment.

Today the American Civil Liberties Union and others who watch the barometer of free speech are concerned about what they call "a new siege of the First Amendment," a rising hostility to freedom of expression. They cite the uproar over Robert Mapplethorpe's photographs, followed by Congress's adoption of Jesse Helms's amendment putting content restrictions on grants to the arts, and then followed by the craven decision of the National Endowment for the Arts to demand a purity oath of artists before helping them. Yes, that was troubling, but I have to say it was hardly novel. Puritanism and intolerance of eccentricity are among the oldest strains in American culture.

When H.L. Mencken railed against "the booboisie" in the 1920's, the examples of censorship were far more absurd. No state today is bringing criminal prosecutions against teachers who tell their students about the theory of evolution. A country in which the Supreme Court says the Reverend Jerry Falwell is constitutionally subject to raucous spoofing by *Hustler* magazine is not under the rule of Ayatollahs. But that does not make me altogether relaxed, nor should it you.

For me, the most worrying First Amendment problem of our time is the growth of secrecy in the federal government. My central concern is with the vitality of the Madisonian premise that we the citizens are the ultimate sovereigns of this country, and are therefore entitled to know what our government is doing and to criticize its characters and measures. That premise is being undermined to a significant degree by official secrecy. What gives me particular concern is that so few of us seem to care about it.

A startling illustration of that unhappy fact is the Iran-contra affair. We do not know all that happened by any means, but we do know that Oliver North and others subverted the Constitution, spending money that Congress had not appropriated for purposes that Congress had explicitly forbidden. Yet the efforts by an independent counsel to bring the conspirators to justice have been thwarted by the Justice Department and the courts. Reasons are given for the obstructions put in the counsel's way: that information cannot be declassified, for example. But I think that underlying the weak response of the legal system to this dangerous lawlessness is the lack of public outrage. People just do not seem to care that operations damaging to our country were carried out in a manner that violated the Madisonian constitutional premise.

I shall end with a comment about a current disturbing phenomenon, and that is the public feeling about the press during the Persian Gulf War. Most people, if I read opinion correctly, thought the press should just do what the military said, stop asking questions, and let the Government get on with the war. That attitude, deference to officials, is what produced such fair and effective government in, say, the Soviet Union or Mengistu's Ethiopia or Pinochet's Chile.

But I suppose we should not be surprised to see some Americans ready to regard questioning as illegitimate. Patriotism has overwhelmed common sense and American principle from time to time in our history. The idea of subjecting government to criticism, the idea that wicked citizens can disagree with their rulers, the idea of an open society always seems to some people, as it did in 1798, a dangerous idea. It is still an experiment, as all life is an experiment. But it is ours.

CHAPTER 1

Censorship and Our Threatened First Amendment

> Congress shall make no law respecting an establishment of religion, or prohibiting the free exercise thereof; or abridging the freedom of speech, or of the press, or the right of the people peaceably to assemble, and to petition the Government for a redress of grievances.

From the beginning of recorded history governments and their agents have engaged in various forms of censorship. Sometimes, the reason given was that the material being censored would endanger national security, life or limb, or property rights (e.g., statutes prohibiting mail fraud or other conduct that is designed to bilk the public). However, more often than not governments have abridged freedom of speech simply because they found such speech to be "offensive." It might offend the religious or political sensibilities of government; it might offend people in power; or, it might offend the moral sensibilities of society. Laws restricting or prohibiting the sale or dissemination of sexually explicit materials fall into this category. Since in recent years such laws have proliferated, we provide here a brief history of censorship of such materials in the United States.

Throughout history, governments have tried to censor or suppress materials that they felt were "seditious" or "heretical." Only in the last 150 years have they concerned themselves seriously with the suppression of sexual materials. Materials that would now be considered pornographic in the extreme were in common circulation in England for centuries. At the end of the sixteenth century, however, the Puritan view (which rejected all pleasure as sinful and immoral) began to gain influence. But even the Puritans failed to define obscenity and they rarely attacked a work unless it was considered anti-religious. It wasn't until 1857 that the English passed a law prohibiting dissemination of obscene materials.

The American colonists adopted most of the great body of statutes and common law that were current in England in the seventeenth century. Included among these were the Tolera-tion Act and the Bill of Rights, which were enacted in England in 1689 as a reflection of the general sentiment against ar-bitrary government. These acts guaranteed certain safeguards to the individual, although freedom of speech was not among them. Sexual materials circulated freely in the colonies. How-ever, in 1711 Massachusetts enacted a law that proscribed the "evil communication" of "profane and obscene" materials, particularly as they were used in "imitation of preaching or any other part of divine worship." No one was prosecuted for violating that statute until 110 years later in 1821.

Government censorship certainly existed during this period and the British laws of libel and slander, which made it a crime to criticize the government, were enforced. But the sentiments that brought about the American Revolution pointed the way to a new spirit and an expanded idea of individual rights. The first ten amendments of the American Bill of Rights, ratified in 1791, guaranteed individual freedoms, notably in the areas of freedom of religion, speech, and the press.

Ultimate responsibility for interpretation of the Constitu-tion and the Bill of Rights, however, lies with the Supreme Court, which has struggled to define the boundaries of the First Amendment for 200 years.

Federal anti-obscenity statutes were passed in the mid-nineteenth century but there was little enforcement until 1868 when Anthony Comstock, a grocery clerk in New York, formed a national organization to ensure that the newly-enacted obscenity legislation in that state was enforced rigorously. So influential was this group that in 1873 Congress broadened the federal mail act and, by 1900, thirty states had statutes of some sort prohibiting dissemination of obscene materials. Throughout this period and through the first fifty years of the 1900's, many books, plays, films, and works of art were suppressed as obscene. The prevailing definition was that set forth in 1868 in an English case, *Queen* v. *Hicklin*, which defined obscenity as that which tended "to deprave and corrupt those whose minds are open to such immoral influences...." This was a landmark decision in that it allowed, for the first time, the suppression of materials solely because of the *sexual* content, unrelated to any attack on religious or governmental institutions.

With each obscenity case that was considered in the following years, the confusion over the definition of obscenity increased. In 1957 the Supreme Court in *Roth* v. *U.S.* rejected the Hicklin definition and ruled that a work could not be judged obscene based on an isolated passage, that the entire work and its possible effect on a "normal" person must be taken into consideration. *Roth* v. *U.S.* held that the First Amendment did not protect obscenity, in that obscenity was without the "slightest redeeming social importance." The Court did, however, declare that sex and obscenity were not synonymous, that "obscene" material caters primarily to the "prurient interest," and that an obscene work must offend "the common conscience of the community by present-day standards." *Alberts* v. *California*, a companion case to Roth, upheld the power of the states to ban obscene materials, effectively narrowing the scope of speech protected by the First Amendment. The definition of "community" continues to be interpreted in a variety of ways. Defendants in obscenity cases tend to push for the broader and generally more tolerant "state" or "national" standard as the appropriate community standard to be observed.

In *Butler* v. *Michigan*, delivered that same year, the Court rejected an attempt by Michigan to prevent distribution of sexually explicit (but not obscene) material to adults to avoid the risk of juveniles being exposed to it. In the opinion of Justice Frankfurter, the result of such a law would be to "reduce the adult population...to reading only what is fit for children."

However, ten years later, the Supreme Court significantly narrowed the interpretation of *Butler* v. *Michigan. Ginsburg* v. *New York* made it a crime to sell material defined as "harmful to minors" (but not obscene for adults) to anyone under the age of seventeen. The Court asserted the power of the state to "protect" children, even if the exercise of that power meant an invasion of constitutionally protected freedoms. In the wake of the Ginsburg ruling, many states began to pass laws. These banned not only the *sale* of sexually explicit materials to minors, but also the *display* of such materials where they would be accessible to minors. States have attempted to require "adults only" shelves and bagging or stapling of books and magazines. The appellate courts have struck down these ordinances repeatedly because they also restrict adult access to constitutionally protected materials.

In 1988 the Supreme Court of the United States had the opportunity in *ABA* v. *Virginia* to determine the constitutionality of minors' access legislation. The State of Virginia had enacted a statute typical of those previously or since enacted in other states. The American Booksellers Association (ABA) and other members of the Media Coalition immediately challenged the statute, meeting with success in the Federal District Court and in the Fourth Circuit Court of Appeals. Virginia appealed to the Supreme Court. Somewhat surprisingly, the Court held that it could not decide upon the constitutionality of the Virginia obscenity statute until it was made aware of the manner in which the State of Virginia might interpret it.

The Court certified two questions to the Supreme Court of Virginia. The first question dealt with the "general standard" to be used to determine the statute's breach in light of the differing ages and levels of maturity of juveniles. The second question asked whether the statute would be complied with "by a plaintiff bookseller who has a policy of not permitting juveniles to examine material covered by the statute and who prohibits such conduct when observed but otherwise takes no action regarding the display of restricted materials." The Virginia Supreme Court answered both questions in the affirmative.

The result, in effect, is that in the State of Virginia the term "harmful to juveniles" is almost indistinguishable from the term "obscene" when it applies to adults. In addition, a bookseller will be in compliance with the statute by simply having a posted policy of not allowing minors to "peruse" books and magazines that are "harmful to juveniles." It remains to be seen whether courts in other states will interpret their obscenity statutes as narrowly as Virginia has in order to avoid a ruling of unconstitutionality. ABA and other members of the Media Coalition are currently in the process of challenging minors' access statutes in Georgia and New Mexico.

The 1960's and the accompanying "sexual revolution" were a relatively permissive time but not everyone was happy about this trend. At the urging of Congress, President Johnson in 1968 appointed an obscenity commission that was to report back in two years on the seriousness of the traffic in pornography and its effects on society. Twelve of the eighteen members of the commission agreed in its final statement that neither state nor federal governments should attempt to regulate sexual materials and that obscenity legislation already in place, except concerning safeguards for minors, should be *repealed*. The commission stated, "Extensive empirical investigation, both by the commission and others, provides no evidence that exposure to or use of explicit sexual materials plays a significant role in the causation of social or individual harms such as crime, delinquency, sexual or nonsexual deviancy, or severe emotional disturbances." And further,

"Governmental regulation of moral choice can deprive the individual of the responsibility for personal decision that is essential to the formation of genuine moral standards. Such regulation would also tend to establish an official moral orthodoxy, contrary to our most fundamental constitutional traditions." President Nixon and the U.S. Senate later repudiated these findings.

In 1973 the Supreme Court formulated a new legal definition of obscenity. In *Miller* v. *California,* the Court set forth these standards that defined obscenity, to wit:

> ...material or a performance that:
>
> (1) The average person, applying contemporary community standards, would find that taken as a whole appeals to the prurient interest in sex;
>
> (2) Depicts or describes: Patently offensive representations or descriptions of ultimate sex acts, normal or perverted, actual or simulated, including sexual intercourse, sodomy, and sexual bestiality; and
>
> (3) Taken as a whole, lacks serious literary, artistic, political, or scientific value.

The use of the word "serious" in (3) is significant. It represents a widening of scope over the Roth wording, which had said that obscenity must be without "the slightest redeeming social value."

Miller and three companion cases dealing with obscenity were decided by a 5-4 vote, with four justices vigorously dissenting. Justices William O. Douglas and Hugo L. Black adhered to their long held positions that it was unconstitutional to have any censorship of offensive ideas. Justice Douglas in his dissent stated, "The idea that the First Amendment permits punishment for ideas that are 'offensive' to the particular judge or jury sitting in judgment is astounding....To give the power to the censor, as we do today, is to make a sharp and radical break with the traditions of a free society." Justice Brennan, the author of the decision *Roth* v. *United States,* stated:

> ...after fifteen years of experimentation and debate I am reluctantly
> forced to the conclusion that none of the available formulas, including
> the one announced today, can reduce the vagueness to a tolerable
> level....[T]he notion that there is a legitimate state concern in the
> "control [of] the moral content of a person's thoughts" is wholly
> inconsistent with the philosophy of the First Amendment.

No discussion of the course of censorship in this country
would be complete without some mention of the "Meese
Commission." In May 1985 Attorney General William French
Smith appointed an eleven-member "Attorney General's
Commission on Pornography," later referred to as the Meese
Commission. The commission held a series of rather
melodramatic hearings featuring testimony by "victims" of
pornography and by police from vice and morals squads who
were testifying as "experts" on child molestation and the harmful effects of pornography. At the end of the series of hearings
the commission finally gave in to pressure and listened to a few
representatives from the book publishing industry and the
library community. The American Booksellers Association
was not permitted to testify despite its requests to do so.

The commission published its findings in July 1986. In its
final report, the commission apologized because, due to severe
budgetary and time restraints, it was unable to test its
hypotheses. Nevertheless, the commission went on to venture
conclusions about the causal relationship between pornography and "antisocial" conduct or even criminal conduct, this
despite the lack of any corroborative evidence linking the two
phenomena and the existence of several reputable studies that
indicated that the majority of the American people was not in
favor of censorship. A minority report submitted by two dissenting members of the commission stated that the "research
has not been designed to evaluate the relationship between
exposure to pornography and the commission of sexual crimes;
therefore, efforts to tease the current data into proof of a
causal link between these acts simply cannot be accepted...."

Pressure from the executive director of the commission
sought to intimidate legitimate businesses, including K-Mart

and the Southland Corporation. A letter on the commission's letterhead accused those businesses of being the nation's largest purveyors of pornography (in that they distributed *Playboy* and *Penthouse* magazines, neither of which contain "obscene" materials). The letter suggested that the stores and distributors who carried the magazines might like to reconsider or be named in the final report as purveyors of pornography. Many stores did succumb to this pressure and removed the magazines from their shelves. *Playboy* and the American Booksellers Association subsequently sued the Meese Commission for these false accusations and won, forcing the commission to withdraw the letter and prohibiting it from publishing the corporation names. It was later shown that the secret testimony of the Reverend Donald Wildmon, founder of the fundamentalist, right wing American Family Association, had led to the commission's illegal actions.

Civil rights groups severely criticized the Meese Commission. They contended that the commission collected insufficient data from biased witnesses and then twisted it to fit their original, unspoken mandate to find a direct correlation between pornography and criminal conduct.

The Meese Commission endorsed a broad new array of law enforcement initiatives, including establishment by the Attorney General of a task force to deal with the problem of obscenity. One of the more extraordinary recommendations of the commission was its encouragement of private individuals to conduct picketing and boycotts to discourage the dissemination of sexually explicit materials, whether or not the First Amendment protected the offending materials. It is arguable that such a recommendation, by a government agency, is itself a violation of the First Amendment.

Another important development and legacy of the Meese Commission has been the use (recommended by the commission) of "Racketeer Influenced and Corrupt Organizations" (RICO) statutes that permit forfeiture of entire businesses because of the publication or sale of obscene materials. Under

RICO, only two instances of purveying obscenity are required to create a "pattern of activity" that could result in forfeiture. As the ABA counsel stated in a brief to the Indiana Court of Appeals in 1987, "...RICO also provides an effective means to eliminate legitimate businesses that may have inadvertently crossed the gray line between what is obscene and what is not, as well as an effective means to coerce legitimate businesses into refraining from stocking or distributing First Amendment-protected material."

In 1987 the owners of a chain of adult bookstores in Virginia were convicted under the federal RICO statutes. The conviction was based upon a finding that they had sold offensive materials for a retail value of $105.30. In addition to jail terms, their entire business, valued at approximately $2 million, was forfeited. On appeal the Fourth Circuit Court of Appeals sustained the conviction and the forfeiture.

During the 1980's a variety of laws was used to purge society of sexually explicit books, magazines, motion pictures, and videotapes. These laws include zoning laws, nuisance laws, expanded minors' access laws (based on broader definitions of "harmful to minors"), book store licensing, and victim's compensation laws. The primary goal of certain legislation is not to restrict access to sexually explicit though constitutionally protected materials. It is instead to improve a neighborhood by use of the method of rezoning. Such legislation is likely to withstand constitutional scrutiny (*Young* v. *American Mini Theatres, Inc.*). However, where legislation is intended to limit the dissemination of sexually explicit but constitutionally protected materials that are demeaning to women, blacks, homosexuals or some other group, such a law is likely to be in violation of the First Amendment (*ABA* v. *Hudnut*). In Hudnut, the ordinance in question was intended to prohibit the sale or dissemination of sexually explicit books, magazines or other materials that were demeaning to women. In a ringing opinion, Judge Sarah Barker of the Federal District Court in Indianapolis held that such legislation had the effect of banning material because of its viewpoint. This the First Amendment will not abide.

The ABA has joined with others in a case against the State of Tennessee, which in the spring of 1990 passed legislation that is extremely restrictive to booksellers concerning display of materials that the state might deem "harmful to minors." Among other provisions, the bill expands the definition of "harmful to minors" to include within its scope both materials with sexual content and material with violent content, thus vastly expanding the range of materials that would have to be removed from display. One of the bills also invokes "public nuisance" laws that allow for seizure or loss of a business.

In January 1990, the Supreme Court ruled against a proposed ordinance to license book stores in Dallas. The Dallas effort to restrict book stores that sell sexually explicit material via a licensing requirement was of course also a threat to mainstream booksellers because it would have endowed a municipality with the power to grant or deny a license to a book store of any kind.

The most recent wrinkle in this seemingly unending censorship struggle is the proliferation of "victim's compensation" laws that began to appear in the wake of convicted killer Ted Bundy's assertion that pornography had motivated his sexual assaults on women. This self-serving declaration of course fanned the coals of zealots' claims that there is a direct cause and effect between pornography and violent crime. The Washington state legislature passed a law that would have permitted an 18 percent tax on any non-obscene material depicting nudity or "sexually explicit" conduct. The Governor, however, agreed with opponents who felt that the definition of sexually explicit was unconstitutionally broad and he vetoed the bill.

Another bill was then introduced that would have permitted lawsuits against booksellers and publishers for selling sexually explicit (but not legally obscene) materials. This proposed bill died in committee but a similar bill did pass in Illinois. These laws would allow the victim of a sexual assault to sue the producer and wholesale distributor of obscene material that is found to be the "proximate cause" of the assault. Similar bills have been introduced in the U.S. Senate.

The Michigan legislature is considering a package of legislation that would make a bookseller or publisher liable for criminal penalties for selling "hard-core" material that is the proximate cause of a sexual assault. The proponents, who say that they want the toughest obscenity laws they can get, are hoping to persuade the Supreme Court to reconsider and to broaden its definition of obscenity. Booksellers in Michigan are not taking this lying down. They have done a phenomenal job of organizing to fight this legislation, including hiring a full-time lobbyist and mounting a massive campaign to educate the public.

Most recently the forces of morality and clean living have been especially creative in conjuring up legislation that will discourage the sale or dissemination of constitutionally protected but sexually explicit books, magazines or other materials. Observing the success that Tipper Gore had in bringing about the voluntary labeling of recordings deemed "harmful to minors," the Louisiana legislature enacted a statute requiring the labeling of recordings, including books on tape, which are sexually explicit, encourage suicide or criminal behavior or encourage other socially unacceptable behavior. Fortunately, Governor Buddy Romer recognized the unconstitutionality of the legislation and vetoed it. However, in the present climate we can expect Louisiana and perhaps other states to enact similar legislation in the not too distant future.

To quote Max Lillienstein, ABA counsel, "It would appear that the forces of morality and clean living have been especially creative during the last year. Every time the Media Coalition succeeds in having a statute or ordinance declared unconstitutional, these forces seem to be able to dream up some other threat to freedom of expression." (The Media Coalition is an association founded in 1973 that defends the First Amendment rights of booksellers, publishers, periodical wholesalers, and distributors in the United States. Its members include the ABA and the Association of American Publishers.)

The most recent federal obscenity law, The Child Protection and Obscenity Enforcement Act of 1988, may pose the most serious threat yet to the publishing and distribution of sexually explicit but non-obscene materials. Among other things, it contains severe criminal penalties and forfeiture provisions that potentially threaten the very survival of a publisher or seller of sexually explicit materials. In an effort to have the law declared unconstitutional, a coalition that included the American Library Association, the Freedom to Read Foundation, and six trade associations filed suit in March 1989 against three top government officials, stating that the Child Protection and Obscenity Enforcement Act represented "...a grave and genuine threat to the First Amendment privileges."

In May 1989, the coalition was successful in having the record-keeping provisions and the provision allowing the seizure of assets before conviction (prior restraint) declared unconstitutional. However, Attorney General Thornburgh appealed the ruling and oral arguments were heard in October 1990 by the United States Circuit Court of Appeals for the District of Columbia.

After a Federal District Court ruled that the above provisions were unconstitutional, Congress passed an amending statute in the waning hours of the 101st Congress, The Child Protection Restoration & Penalties Enhancement Act of 1990. In this act, Congress corrected many of the unconstitutional abuses that might have emanated from the original statute, but unfortunately added amendments that even further muddy the constitutional waters. The American Booksellers Foundation for Free Expression will be paying close attention to the 1988 statute and the 1990 amendment in the months and years ahead.

Armed with a knowledge of the social and legislative history of the First Amendment and of the forms that censorship has taken over the years, individuals and groups should not hesitate to challenge those who would try to stifle the free and open exchange of ideas that is essential to the preservation of our democracy.

This chapter was prepared by Lisa Knudsen, of the Mountains and Plains Booksellers Association, with the assistance of ABA counsel Max Lillienstein, of Cooperman Levitt & Winikoff, P.C., New York, NY.

CHAPTER 2

American Psycho:
A Case Study

W hen Vintage published *American Psycho* by Bret Easton Ellis in March 1991, it sparked a media debate the impact of which was felt on the sales floors of book stores around the country. As a recent and high-profile instance of controversy that raised the hackles of both right and left, the book provides an opportune example of the many issues involved in the debate over censorship.

The American Booksellers Foundation for Free Expression (ABFFE) responded to the outcry over *American Psycho* by distributing helpful information to booksellers around the country. This material included answers to frequently asked questions and a sample media/public statement. Reprinted at the end of this chapter, that information can serve as a model in dealing with controversial books in the future.

As an experienced bookseller, Joyce Meskis, of the Tattered Cover book store in Denver and American Booksellers Association President, contributes several practical tips for booksellers. Her essay on free expression, excerpted below from *American Bookseller* magazine (March 1991), reinforces the importance of booksellers in protecting the First Amendment.

SPEAKING OUT FOR FREE EXPRESSION

Just when I think I've experienced every scenario possible in bookselling regarding stocking "offensive" (controversial) books, another one comes along. I remember years ago the stir over the publication of *Peyton Place*; the challenge by a parent about *Coming of Age in Samoa* and *The Joy of Sex*. *Fascinating Womanhood* came under attack from time to time, as did *The Insanity Defense and the Trial of John Hinckley*, perceived by some to be promoting political assassination.

Although we have always spent considerable time discussing the censorship issue and the store's stand in relation to it, while interviewing and training new employees we can never quite cover all the possibilities or predict the responses. Inevitably, when we think of censorship issues, we think of "banned in Boston," *Ulysses*, and *Lady Chatterley's Lover*, yet today the challenges seem more complex and often unanticipated.

What bookseller could have foreseen that our working lives would be touched by not only the threat, but the act, of terrorism? The publication of *The Satanic Verses* unleashed a whole new modus operandi, and a whole new set of emotions in response to it.

A recent addition to the long history of controversial books was *American Psycho*. The degree of media attention focused on its publication triggered an intense public reaction. The national response involved picketing and a boycott called for by the Los Angeles Chapter of the National Organization for Women. At our store, customers had questions and comments about the book, and there were requests from the press for statements of position.

While I continue to look for new ways to deal more effectively with these situations in our own store, I have learned a few things over the years that seem to help in defusing difficult confrontations.

1. Get an early start on clarifying your store's position in your own mind.

2. Prepare a few short sentences that clearly state your position—and that you can remember, even during the most heated exchange. (However, see the fifth point....) Be sure to avoid language that sounds defensive.

3. Involve your staff. Listen to their thoughts and suggestions. Discuss the issue with them so that they understand the reasoning behind the decision to provide readers with access to controversial material. While not everyone may be in complete agreement, be clear that the expectation is that each staff member will be able to articulate briefly the store's position. Designate an official spokesperson, usually the owner or general manager. This person can be called upon to communicate with the media and to handle the more potentially volatile exchanges with upset customers. This assures a consistent presentation. The customer, too, is more likely to feel heard. The staff member may simply state that it's the store's policy to provide an uncensored environment where ideas of all kinds are available, thereby protecting the reader's right to choose. Such a statement can then be followed with one noting that the manager would very much like to hear the customer's thoughts.

4. If possible, try to prepare a written handout, an effective way of communicating your store's position with customers and the media. A good start is the one-page statement reproduced at the end of this chapter.

5. When confronted with angry customers, listen to them with respect. Respond briefly, clearly, and unequivocally in a cool, rational manner. This isn't the setting for extended debate, but clear analogies are often useful, such as pointing out that there is an infinite number of special interest groups, many of which would like to prevent the public distribution of various materials. Thank the customers for sharing their opinions, even if you wind up agreeing to disagree. Depending on the situation, you may want to follow up an exchange with a letter, offering a more extensive explanation.

6. Dealing with the media can be even more difficult. Words have to be chosen very carefully, as does the order in which they're presented, so that they are not likely to be taken out of context. The editing process can sometimes present a dis-

torted point of view. I have noticed, too, that it's not uncommon to be asked unrelated questions. There's nothing wrong with ignoring such questions and bringing the discussion back to the point—censorship—not, for instance, the literary merits of a particular book.

7. Take a breath and realize that you are not alone in your point of view. While such challenges can be very disquieting, booksellers have discovered that there are a great many individuals in communities nationwide opposed to censorship.

Standing firm in support of the First Amendment isn't an easy thing to do. The bookseller can feel caught in what, at times, seems to be a web of concerns: the image of the store in the community, staff opinion, personal choices. Choice is what it's all about, isn't it? Certainly the bookseller has a First Amendment right to project the business image of his or her choice. Few would argue the point. Yet, I would contend that a person when making the decision to become a bookseller should set aside those personal proclivities, those literary prejudices, and, yes, those moralistic judgments in the interest of a higher good—the free exchange of ideas.

Now, that's not to say that we don't all have our own sacred cows, those issues close to our own special interests that trigger strong reactions. Yet, we took on a special responsibility when we made the decision to become booksellers. In a very real sense, we booksellers are gatekeepers of the free expression of ideas. It's my view that as booksellers we have our own version of the Hippocratic oath—to maintain the health and well-being of the First Amendment.

QUESTIONS AND ANSWERS ON
AMERICAN PSYCHO

Q. Should I stock *American Psycho*?

A. As a bookseller this is your decision entirely. Under our constitutional system, you have the right to offer for sale whatever constitutionally protected material you may choose.

However, you are by no means compelled to offer any work to the public either. Under the First Amendment, such decisions regarding free expression are yours to make.

Q. Is a controversial work such as *American Psycho* protected by the Constitution?

A. Only if *American Psycho* is adjudicated to be obscene in a court of law does it lose its First Amendment protection. Under the guidelines set forth by the 1973 *Miller* v. *California* case, it is highly unlikely that a work such as *American Psycho* would be legally obscene.*

Q. From what I've read or seen in the media, some people have very strong feelings about this book. If I decide to carry it in my store, how can I respond to customers who may question its sale?

A. First off—though it can sometimes be unpleasant to have a customer question a decision you've made—remind yourself that the same First Amendment that protects your freedom as a bookseller also protects anyone's right to express his/her opinion. So listen to them with respect. However, the sales floor on a working day isn't the setting for an extended debate. So, respond succinctly and clearly in explaining that you believe your role as a bookseller is to offer for sale a wide array of legal titles containing ideas as diverse as the community in which you live.

Q. What if a customer argues that *American Psycho* isn't "worth" having in the store?

A. Stress in your response that your role as a bookseller is not that of a critic. While any particular book may not be to your taste, as a bookseller you will never stand in the way of your customer's right to read.

---

* Under the 1973 *Miller* v. *California* decision, to prove that a work is legally obscene it must meet all of the following criteria: a. Appeals primarily to prurient interest; b. Must be patently offensive to the community; c. Must lack serious literary, artistic, political, and scientific value.

Q. How should I respond to questions from the media?

A. Your explanation is really not any different. Within the context of your store you may want to refer all media calls to the owner or manager, primarily to stay abreast of the number and type of inquiries. You may also want to produce a one-page statement that can be given to media and customers explaining your store's commitment to the First Amendment and the rights of free expression. (See sample statement at the end of this chapter.)

Q. What if people picket or protest in other ways at the store?

A. Again, remember that so long as their protests don't violate any local ordinances or state laws (you should check with your local police department), they have a right to promote a point of view in support of or in opposition to any book. However, others do not have the right to interfere with anyone having access to a particular book because they may find it offensive. Nor do they have the right to suggest that because one title may be particularly distasteful booksellers ought to deny access to thousands of other titles from any publisher.

Q. Isn't picketing/boycotting a cherished part of the American right to dissent?

A. Certainly. However, the ABFFE Board of Directors believes that pickets/boycotts directed against books are distinct from those aimed at most consumer products. While other products are replaceable, the ideas contained in any one book are not. Any effort that attempts to interfere with access to those ideas is contrary to what the First Amendment and free speech are all about.

Q. Will pickets affect my business?

A. Since only a very tiny percentage of people usually participates in public protests of this kind, there are rarely long-term adverse effects if the situation is handled in a straightforward manner. However, if pickets appear at your store, you would be well advised to seek legal advice to ascertain if the picketing is being conducted in a legal manner.

Q. Where can I turn for help?

A. Many, many places. The majority of your community supports your right to sell a wide range of First Amendment protected works. Within your community, you will find booksellers, librarians, writers, and others who will want to work with you in promoting the First Amendment. Very often, some of your own customers can be your strongest supporters. On the national level, the American Booksellers Association established the American Booksellers Foundation for Free Expression specifically to respond to these sorts of situations. A list of other national organizations concerned with censorship issues is also included in this handbook.

A SAMPLE MEDIA/PUBLIC STATEMENT

As a bookseller, I believe that buying a book or not buying a book; voicing or not voicing opinion about the merits of a book are legitimate acts expressing a First Amendment right.

However, organizing an effort that inhibits the distribution of constitutionally protected materials to the reading public or that chills an environment where they may be made available clearly interferes with the rights of others to have access to those materials. Boycotts, demonstrations, and picket lines at bookstores serve to chill the air that allows the free flow of ideas in our society. Such actions potentially restrict the availability of a significant number of titles based on the pressure exerted by a group that has a special interest in promoting its own standards on the community. Even when there may be agreement by the majority, the importance of holding safe the access to unpopular ideas has been demonstrated historically.

Book stores and libraries are "houses of ideas" and should be respected as such, nurtured and supported so that information may continue to flow freely in our society. It is the right of the reader to make the choice, to read or not to read, to buy or not to buy a certain book. But a generalized boycott of ideas is not like a boycott of any other product. The economic impact may bear similarities, but the real bottom line when it comes to books is that speech, debate, and ultimately thought will be limited.

CHAPTER 3

Getting Things Done: Working with Lawyers, Lobbyists, and Public Officials

T his chapter offers guidelines and suggestions for how to deal with and make use of the people who will be your most important resources, allies, and adversaries in the struggle to protect your First Amendment rights as a bookseller.

LAWYERS

The times a book store is most likely to need the services of a lawyer in matters of free expression are: (1) when charged under a city or state ordinance for displaying or selling materials judged in that jurisdiction to be obscene or harmful to minors; and (2) when a store or group of stores decides to challenge such an ordinance. In either case, having the proper lawyer is essential.

● Several types of violations of your civil liberties give good grounds for successful lawsuits. The overriding consideration is that you or your organization must personally have suffered the infringement.

● Talk to American Booksellers Association legal counsel and Media Coalition legal counsel. They can tell you what qualifications are important in order for a lawyer to meet your needs and constitute an important resource if you have a sudden need for a lawyer.

• Get referrals and recommendations from other businesses, retail colleagues, or other contacts. Consider finding a good lawyer *before* you need one, so you'll be prepared when you need one in a hurry.

• Keep in mind that some of your customers may be lawyers who work in the community. Getting to know these people, discussing matters of free expression, and learning about their views and expertise may be of future use.

• Look for lawyers with constitutional law/applicable law experience. Many lawyers do not know that much about this area. Take time to find out which lawyers belong to the American Civil Liberties Union (ACLU).

• Another option is to go to your local library or to any local lawyer's office and ask to see the *Martindale Hubble Bar Register*, an encyclopedia of lawyers, for your area. This is a multi-volume reference that includes the name and area of practice of almost any reputable lawyer. If you end up with several names, check the beginning of the volume, which contains a rating of most attorneys: "av" signifies the highest caliber.

• Nearly any lawyer will allow you to conduct an initial interview or consultation at no cost or at relatively low cost to discuss your case and matters of expense.

• Establish fees and expenses right away. Discuss your budget and set specific limits up front. The total cost of a case is dependent upon the amount of time the lawyers must spend in taking depositions, doing research, preparing briefs, and pleading the case. It is essential that you determine from the outset exactly what a lawyer will do and at what price. Keep in mind that you should use the lawyer cost-efficiently. If you take care of routine matters yourself (copying, for example), it will cost you far less.

• ACLU and other organizations will at times take on the costs of a case. In these cases, lawyers have volunteered to do the work pro bono and are normally selected by that organization. Your lawyer may be willing to work for a contingent fee, meaning he or she only gets paid if you win. Or your lawyer may be willing to contribute services because of the important issues involved.

• Educate the lawyer regarding your issues and your position on them. An important aspect of the initial session with your lawyer is the discussion of your position in the case. Try to be as clear and concise as you can. It is crucial that the lawyer not only have the pertinent facts but also your personal position regarding the circumstances of the case. For example, if you have chosen to carry materials which are protected by the First Amendment although they may violate a local ordinance, it is important that your lawyer know how and why you made that decision and the fact that you believe that the ordinance violates the First Amendment. However, if you are genuinely confused about the laws involved, legal procedures, etc., say so immediately and ask plenty of questions until you feel satisfied with your understanding of the matter.

• Consider the lawyer's advice regarding the viability of your position. Expect that he or she will tell you plenty you would rather not hear, but be sure that you have a basic comfort level with the quality of the advice and its applicability to your case.

• Keep your lawyer well-informed of the ongoing details of your situation. Pass on information on a timely basis, and be certain that your lawyer does the same for you.

LOBBYISTS

When you hire a lobbyist, the main things you are acquiring are access and experience. They provide access to the power brokers and experience in influencing legislation: what points to make, when to make them, how to make them, who should make them, etc. A good lobbyist will not only be working on your behalf, he or she will give you advice that will help you use your limited time, money, and energy to the best advantage.

● There are two kinds of lobbyists: those who are employed by an organization and lobby exclusively for that organization; and multi-client lobbyists, who are self-employed and contract their services to a client. You will likely be considering a multi-client firm.

● There are two options for hiring a lobbyist: on retainer or for single-issue lobbying.

   ● The advantage of single-issue is that once the issue of concern (e.g., a piece of censorship legislation) is resolved, you terminate the relationship with the lobbyist and avoid additional costs. The disadvantage of that method is that it won't be as effective as the same lobbyist working on retainer. It takes time for client and lobbyist to get to know each other. It also takes time for the lobbyist to really understand the range of the client's concerns. Finally, and equally important, it takes time for the legislators and bureaucrats to become aware that the lobbyist represents your group and that you make up a constituency they need to take seriously.

   ● The advantage of a retainer arrangement is that over time, you and the lobbyist get to know each other and your needs. In addition, the legislators and bureaucrats will understand immediately that your lobbyist speaks for you. As you develop a legislative presence, you cannot only work to ward off damaging legislation, but begin to propose helpful legislation. The disadvantage is that you build in substantial ongoing costs.

● What kinds of things will a lobbyist do for you? A full-service firm can do a great deal, including secretarial work, newsletters, mailings, etc., all at a charge, of course. The following would be typical services: monitoring legislation; providing analyses of legislation that needs attention; developing a strategy for "working" the issues (this might include a grass-roots campaign and a public campaign as well as the behind-the-scenes work that the lobbyists themselves do); providing periodic status reports; giving advice on how to approach legislators; and helping to prepare testimony.

● Consider finding a lobbyist before you need one, so you'll be prepared when you need one in a hurry.

● Get referrals and recommendations from other businesses. The best source of information is legislative aides, if you know any who are sympathetic to your issues. They deal with lobbyists all the time, know which ones are most effective, and know who their clients are.

● Look for lobbyists with experience compatible with your store's or organization's needs. Try to be certain the issue at hand is one for which a lobbyist can be useful, such as pending legislation or legislation you would like to see introduced.

● Interview more than one lobbyist. Try to cover the same ground in all interviews so you can be comparing apples to apples. Conduct the interviews with several members of your store or organization so that you can compare perceptions and judgments. Among the issues that should be addressed:

   ● Is the lobbyist already aware of the issues at hand?

   ● Do they have a personal interest in seeing your side prevail? (Helpful, but not necessary.)

   ● Do they have other clients who would be opposing your viewpoint? What would they do if, at some later point, they found their own clients at odds on an issue?

- Do they have other clients who would also be lobbying from your side of the issue? (This might be an advantage in making sure the lobbyist is up to speed, but it could also cause problems in case there is divergence on specific aspects of the issue.)

- Will they supply you with a list of their clients that you might call?

● Establish fees and expenses. Make clear what your budgetary limits are.

● Establish which member of the firm will be handling you.

● Which one to hire? In addition to the obvious considerations of chemistry, budget, commitment to the issues, and proven track record, you should consider the following: in working issues, the more lobbyists on the job, the greater the chance for success. For example, if the librarians, booksellers, record stores, and video stores each have a lobbyist working on an issue, the effect is likely to be considerably greater than if one lobbyist representing all four is working the issue. Everything else being roughly equal, you might want to spread the work around.

● Talk to the American Booksellers Foundation for Free Expression President, American Booksellers Association legal counsel, and Media Coalition legal counsel for a back-up opinion. They can also tell you what qualifications are important in order for a lobbyist to meet your needs.

● Keep in mind that hiring a lobbyist does not mean there is no work for you to do. No matter how persuasive the lobbyist is, it won't help much in tough decisions if the legislator is not convinced that the lobbyist speaks for a constituency that needs to be reckoned with. You will need to be able to get members to make legislative contacts, write letters, and make phone calls at the appropriate moment.

ELECTED AND PUBLIC OFFICIALS

Most elected officials want to do the popular thing. When people are vocal, officials often respond. Therefore, it is important that you be vocal on issues of free expression before a time of crisis.

• Find out in advance, before any trouble arises, who all of your representatives are (city council, state legislature, Congress, etc.). Call the main Capitol telephone number, (202) 224-3121, to determine who represents you in Congress. The operator will ask your address and will have the information for you within a few seconds. You can also try the League of Women Voters at (800) 836-6975. Keep names, addresses, and phone numbers on file for easy access.

• Write your senators at the Senate Office Building, Washington, DC 20510. Write your representative at the House Office Building, Washington, DC 20515. Letters should be as personal as possible. Avoid writing a general or computer-generated letter. Tell those in Congress that you will be monitoring their votes on First Amendment issues, and that *you* will vote accordingly. Be informative as well as emotional. Politicians need to know that you feel strongly about censorship issues. Remember, members of Congress represent you whether or not you voted for them— whether or not you even voted. Elected officials probably fear you. You're their boss. Take advantage of your political power by demanding action to preserve the Bill of Rights.

• Call and get names of aides and assistants to elected officials; find out who does what; establish contact in advance and on an ongoing basis so that these people can be more helpful to you when you really need them.

● It is especially important to write or call when major censorship-related issues are presented as new laws or budget matters. Do your best to learn the title of proposed legislation, or the House or Senate bill number it is going under. (Often, these can be gathered from newspaper articles.)

● Educate yourself regarding the basic workings of the city council, legislature, etc., such as when and where meetings are held, and when public testimony is allowed.

● Find out who can provide you with information—copies of ordinances, laws, agendas for meetings, etc. On a local basis, try the city clerk, city attorney, or council member's office. On a state level, try your representative's office.

● Be persistent in getting the information you need. It often takes numerous tries. Cultivate behind-the-scenes contacts to help you in this.

● Make frequent contact with pertinent elected officials regarding the issue which concerns you. Call, write letters, and set up meetings. Have your fellow booksellers, retail colleagues, and customers follow suit.

● Stay on target with your *professional* focus on the issues. In censorship cases, often those supporting restrictive laws couch the debate in terms of morality. Don't allow them to get you caught up in a *personal* position on the issues.

● If you are dealing with the police, check with your lawyer immediately regarding what actions against you are really legal or illegal. Be prepared to stand up for your rights.

This chapter was prepared by James Dana of The Bookman, Grand Haven, MI, Chuck Robinson of Village Books, Bellingham, WA, and Susan Walker of the Upper Midwest Booksellers Association.

CHAPTER 4

A Case of Anti-Censorship Action That Worked

Deborah Garman, former executive director of the Pacific Northwest Booksellers Association, recently had her first taste of lobbying on behalf of freedom of expression and First Amendment rights. What follows is her dispatch from the front:

As preface to this story, I should introduce myself as an average citizen, generally loaded to maximum capacity with the details of job, homeownership, and family. Although reasonably politically aware on the national and international fronts (I tune in daily to our public radio station), local and state politics had seemed pretty penny-ante stuff. Generally aware, but inactive on all fronts. Membership in the Nature Conservancy, the Sierra Club, and the American Civil Liberties Union (ACLU) served as my manifestations of political energy; there was neither time nor energy for more personal involvement in shaping the world I inhabit.

In early 1991, because of my job as the executive director of the regional booksellers association, I suddenly encountered the importance of politics on the state level. My chosen state of Oregon has now elected legislators who introduced a wide variety of bills intended to limit the civil rights of its citizens. I was particularly shocked by HB2669, a bill written to allow parents of minors to sue booksellers and others who furnished material with pornographic content to their children.

Word arrived that the bill would have a hearing on a day in March that I would be in Idaho administering a small conference for booksellers. Greg Millard, a local bookseller living in the capital city of Salem, had volunteered previously to be the Oregon representative on the regional association's free speech committee. His understanding of that role was that he would watch the newspapers for word on possible problem bills. Expanding his "job description," I asked him to attend the hearing and report back.

One of the first lessons of politics became clear when Greg waited for hours as the subcommittee discussed various bills, then had to leave before "our" hearing to take care of book store business. Greg left a written statement as a bookseller in opposition to the bill. We did get a report from a video store owner who waited long enough to testify against the bill. The word was that enough questions had been raised in testimony that the committee agreed to provide time for another hearing before making a decision on passing the bill to the House floor.

As a result of this hearing in the House Judiciary Committee Family Justice Subcommittee, the Motion Picture Association of America (MPAA) encouraged their lobbyist to negotiate major amendments to the bill. A conscious choice of strategy was made to intervene and collaborate with those supporting the bill. The bill's proponent was a conservative young Democrat named Kevin Mannix, who proved interested in negotiating amendments to the content to ensure his bill's ultimate success. At the national level, the MPAA spent a lot of money and time to provide Representative Mannix with substantive changes to make his bill into better law.

Other concerned groups, including video dealers, booksellers, and librarians, waited and watched for the next hearing, at which they would have an opportunity to express their opposition. Meanwhile, I was doing homework: learning names and phone numbers, and getting the general lay-of-the-land around the State Capitol. I often called Chris Finan at the Media Coalition in New York. He is a tremendous resource.

Throughout the experience, he provided me with support, legal consultation, and suggestions for action. Because of Finan's contacts with representatives of the Video Software Dealers Association (VSDA) and the MPAA at the national level, I had access to all the behind-the-scenes information provided to the MPAA by their lobbyist in Salem. Otherwise, it can be very difficult for a citizen to have a clear idea of the nuances of powerbrokering and dealing going on in the capitol. I developed a close alliance with a local video store owner, Tom Hull. He had a neighbor who had been a senatorial aide. That neighbor was able to provide us with very valuable suggestions about the people and the process determining the fate of HB2669.

The next hearing came on April 17. I screwed up my courage and decided that I would go and perhaps testify. Because of contacts tuned in during the wait, I knew beforehand that the bill had been completely rewritten to change existing criminal law. The amended bill was not available until the moment of the hearing. In fact, the copy handed to me as I entered the hearing room was outdated an hour later when the hearing on the bill began. The bill was now a fairly carefully crafted change to the Oregon criminal statutes dealing with furnishing and displaying material with sexual content to minors. A staff lawyer from the MPAA in Washington, D.C., had actually written the bill and had faxed it to Kevin Mannix. Mannix had used most, but not all, of the provided language. He was sure that he had MPAA/VSDA approval now, and opposition to his bill was gone.

For a layperson like myself, it was a scramble to digest the changes in order to testify, and I was reluctant to do so. Tom Hull was game to testify, and his energy helped me to go ahead. I found the committee to be interested and pleasant, except for Kevin Mannix. My lack of verbal polish was not a problem, and the experience was good for me. Both Hull and I raised problems with specific details of language in the amended bill that were out of line with the national standards of *Miller* v.

California and *Ginsberg* v. *New York*. Based on our suggestions, the committee dropped several words and changed some language. The committee passed the bill to the House with a "do pass" recommendation. The House, with Republicans holding a slim majority for the first time in years, passed the bill overwhelmingly within a few days.

When Chris Finan got a copy of the amended bill, he pointed out that the provisions for display of materials with sexual content were unconstitutional and unacceptable. In looking at the current Oregon criminal statutes, it was clear that HB2669 would tighten and improve the flagrantly unconstitutional language of the current law. In fact, the current law is unenforceable because of its unconstitutionality, and therefore prosecuting attorneys have no usable tool to go after offenders purveying obscenity. Mannix had brought in a district attorney to testify in support of his bill in the committee hearings. What we had in HB2669A (amended) was something better than the existing law, but still unconstitutionally vague. In the hands of an inexperienced or aggressive prosecuting attorney, the new law could be used to criminally prosecute a bookseller selling constitutionally protected books like Henry Miller titles or *The Joy of Sex*.

The work that Representative Kevin Mannix put into amending the bill and making it definitely better than existing law and "almost constitutional" was key to the surprising events which later took place in the Senate. After passage in the House, the bill landed in the Senate Judiciary Committee for review. When Chris Finan's concerns about the bill's display provisions and continued unconstitutionality became clear, I called the executive director of the Oregon ACLU to get the scoop on the Senate Judiciary Committee. She confirmed other bits of opinion that this committee was a group of solidly Democratic protectors of constitutional freedoms. The educated good guess was that this committee would not approve any bills that were unconstitutional in light of the First Amendment.

Somewhat complacent with that news, I waited for the legislative session to end. I checked with Chris Finan from time to time, and he was inactive as well. He was acting in compliance with the MPAA, which had asked that Finan maintain a low profile while their lobbyist monitored the bill, and applied just the right nudges to keep it buried. More often than not, public outcry is seen as inimical to the work of the professional lobbyist. When a lobbyist is at work, he or she hopes to "shoot the dog, but not where the dog's owner can see it happen." Egos and political tit-for-tat play a formidable role in the process.

As the end of the legislative session approached, news coverage indicated that the forty-eight-hour notice of committee hearings had been changed to one-hour notice. This session was problematic for all the legislators because a tremendous amount of time had been spent dealing with repercussions of a property tax cut the voters had passed in the last election. Hundreds of bills were unresolved as the last couple of weeks of the session came on.

What an unpleasant surprise to be notified at 10:30 A.M. on June 11 by someone at the state library that a 1:00 P.M. hearing on HB2669 was scheduled that day! I called Greg Millard in Salem to ask that he take the time to be present and perhaps testify. He agreed. Chris Finan was furious that he had effectively been silenced when he—and the rest of us—could have been contacting the senators on the committee. Tom Hull had a ruptured disc and was unable to drive to Salem. There was no time to mobilize, only to gnash teeth.

Greg reported back that the work session on 2669 had been delayed a day. A reprieve! Chris Finan and I attacked our keyboards and faxed letters to Greg to take into the session on the twelfth. That session had a three-page agenda of bills to consider. After a three hour wait, Greg returned to minding his store without seeing action on our bill.

What happened was a disaster for us. The bill was amended and sent to the Senate floor with a recommendation to pass.

Tom Hull and I spent a great deal of time working to reconstruct and interpret what had happened within the confines of the hearing to convince correct-thinking liberal Democrats that this was acceptable as law. The details became clearer with information from Tom Hull's senator, and after I spent time with the staff person who had administered the hearing. Apparently, the issues were threefold: Kevin Mannix was at the hearing in full power-on mode; the senators were under pressure because there existed the threat that a ballot initiative would be unleashed to amend the state constitution (making pornographic expression *not* protected speech) if some law was not passed to address minors' access issues; and the statements and amendments provided by the two ACLU participants (including the executive director of the Oregon chapter) led the committee to believe that the law was constitutional.

The senate staff administrator seemed to think that there had been little opposition to the bill since he had followed standard procedure and had contacted everyone who had testified against it in earlier hearings. When I pointed out that I had testified earlier and had not been notified formally of the hearing, he became defensive. Since Tom Hull had testified twice previously and had also not been notified, I would guess that mistakes were made.

It was on Thursday, June 13, that word came about the committee's pass recommendation. That day and the next were spent in multiple phone calls to research, clarify, and comprehend the situation. Chris Finan's support was invaluable; Tom Hull's position was that perhaps it really was better law and acceptable given that the MPAA had worked so hard with Representative Mannix. We all had real questions about the ACLU's role at the hearing. Chris Finan was astounded by the ACLU's having provided amendments which still didn't make the bill constitutional. I had a late-breaking brainstorm: I knew a bookseller who had served two terms as a representative in Salem. When I called Nancy Peterson at her book store in

Ashland, she was shocked and dismayed at the news. Her feeling was that at such a late stage, chances were bleak for a turnaround on the Senate floor. Nevertheless, she offered to do all she could with her contacts in the Senate. This included writing a letter in opposition to the bill that she felt she could get carried onto the Senate floor.

Over the weekend, my depression turned to determination to fight as hard as possible in the endgame. On Friday, Chris Finan had offered his assistant, Anne Castro, to make phone calls to booksellers in Oregon to get them calling their senators if I could get him a list. He also passed on the word that the lobbyist for the MPAA in Salem was willing to help organize a phone-in campaign. First thing on Monday morning, I checked in with the lobbyist's office. The lobbyist informed me that the best tactic would be to emphasize business issues for small retailers rather than the philosophical issues of the First Amendment. Common sense and previous experience confirmed this strategy, and the lobbyist's office offered to coach any retailer who phoned them prior to calling their senator. I next called Powell's Bookstore to ask for previously offered assistance on the phoning, faxed a page of my list to Media Coalition, and started down my list of phone calls. I attempted to enlist help from an antiquarian bookseller association, but found they were not organized enough to help. In continuing dialogue with Tom Hull, I helped to nudge him off the fence and back into action phoning his video store owners to organize their calls to senators. I contacted regional coordinators for the Walden and Dalton chains and urged them to alert their Oregon employees to the issue. With six of us administering a "phone tree," almost every book store in Oregon and many of the active video stores were urged to call their senators. It was a gruelling day, especially since it seemed too late, that this was doomed to be wasted energy.

One very important happening was that I got a call back from a new and dedicated bookseller who had made her call. She had just heard back from her senator's office. The message she got from the senator was that the ACLU had endorsed the bill—it was constitutional—and therefore the senator was going to vote to pass the bill. This dovetailed with information from Tom Hull's senator (on the judiciary committee) that Hull and I hadn't entirely been able to digest. Whatever the intentions of the ACLU, it was clear that the members of the judiciary committee *thought* they had heard the ACLU endorse the bill. I had called my ACLU contacts after the committee hearing. They had assured me that the ACLU maintained a formal position in opposition to the bill. Nevertheless, it was obvious that there was damaging confusion about what the ACLU had said to that committee.

During the day, Chris Finan and I discussed the potential role of the Governor in vetoing the bill, as well as possible media attention to the issue to nudge senators and the Governor. I had called local radio and newspaper contacts as I thought of them, and got a mixed reaction. At the end of the legislative session much bigger stories were breaking minute-by-minute. There was not a lot of interest from anyone except the publisher of Portland's *Willamette Week*, a weekly newspaper. A public radio reporter told me quite frankly that they had bigger kettles of fish to fry. More discouragement, along with the realization that grooming contacts in the media should be an important future organizational tactic.

I decided to go for broke and give personal citizen lobbying a try. Armed with yet another round of opposition letters from Media Coalition and the Pacific Northwest Booksellers Association, I drove to the Capitol on Tuesday morning. My knees got pretty weak as I asked where to find the Senate offices, and I felt very much the insignificant cog in the political machine. I felt like turning tail but marched to the elevator instead. My best guess at tactics took me to my own senator's office first, where I should be assured of a reasonably courteous welcome. In fact, this turned out to be the case. The aide there was very helpful and attentive to my statements about the bill. She also was able to pinpoint that the day set for the bill's hearing on the Senate floor would be Thursday. We had been very nervous about the hectic pace of end-of-session events, and had thought that the bill might show up as early as Tuesday, so this was some relief.

The senators were busy in session. I spent the day button-holing aides and staffers in every senator's office and leaving my opposition letter packets. What was tremendously gratifying was to hear that staffers were aware that calls had been coming in about this bill. I saw several tiny yellow post-it notes (each one representing a constituent comment) attached to each senator's HB2669 file folder. I got some positive feedback, and I got some brush-offs. Early on, I stopped at the office of Frank Roberts, a great long-term liberal senator married to the Governor. His staffers were interested and very helpful. They mentioned that the ACLU position was critical to the bill's outcome. The staffers mentioned that perhaps the ACLU should be asked to clarify their position before the floor vote on the bill. What an idea!

My ACLU staff contact was out of town, so I screwed up my courage, went to a pay phone, and called the Oregon ACLU executive director to explain the situation. She spent a few minutes encouraging me to think that this law really was an okay thing compared with what currently existed on the books. I argued that I preferred unenforceable bad law. Apparently, we didn't convince each other, but agreed we were still "on the same side." I asked whether the ACLU's formal stance was that this law was constitutional. She said no. I asked if she could please set into motion a clarification of that point to the full Senate. She agreed to see what she could do.

I then sought out the senator's staffer who had returned my bookseller's call. When the staffer indicated that the ACLU had stamped the bill constitutional, I said I had just heard the contrary from the executive director. Wheels seemed to be set into motion and, exhausted, I went home.

Within twenty-four hours, word came that the ACLU's most active lobbyist had faxed a position statement in opposition to

HB2669 to all senators. Whoopdedoo! Calls continued to filter into senators' offices, and we waited for the floor vote on Thursday, with fingers crossed that it just might be possible that the bill would be sent back to the judiciary committee. Behind the scenes, a senator friend of bookseller Nancy Peterson had set up the paperwork processes to make this a viable option at the time of the floor vote.

Thursday was a tense day and then the phone call came with the word that HB2669 had **BEEN SENT BACK TO COMMITTEE BY A NINETEEN TO TEN VOTE!!** What a personal high that was! Tom Hull and I had a bit of champagne, congratulations went out to all those who had helped, and then we all settled into the countdown to the end of the session. It would be then and only then that we could be absolutely sure that the bill was dead and gone. (At least in this round—we know there will be more to come.)

Word filtered back to our new "coalition" that Kevin Mannix was still pressing for the success of his bill. I got a call from one of his staffers asking what I would like to see "fixed" for booksellers. He said there were plans for several further amendments, and that they would like to make us happy. After the botched experience with the MPAA helping Mannix to do his work, I played very close-lipped. I gave him nothing but a statement on booksellers' distaste for the underlying principle of legislating minors' morality when responsibility should lie with parents and family. He apparently also went back to the national MPAA office with the same request for help in crafting a bill more acceptable to them, but they indicated they also were not interested in working any further with him. More news came in that Mannix had asked the ACLU to do another clarification statement, and that he had roughed up the MPAA lobbyist by whom he seemed to feel betrayed.

Mannix was clearly applying substantial pressure through his channels, so I attempted to maintain equal and opposite pressure on the judiciary committee chairman. I asked a Powell's spokesperson to call, because that was my retailer with the biggest clout. I requested that a bookseller from the committee chairman's district keep inquiry calls going in to the chairman, and I made calls myself on behalf of the association. I sent one final letter of opposition to the chairman's office, indicating that booksellers would not be cowed by the threat of a ballot initiative attacking pornographic speech. I made regular calls to the staff office that organized the judiciary committee work agenda, some calls to the chairman's office, and calls to check in with offices of senators who were sympathetic to our cause. Tom Hull made his calls, we compared notes, and we waited.

Ten tense days passed, with many phone calls occurring daily to check for any news of work scheduled in committee on the bill. The legislative session finished on June 30 without further action. We had won!

Our next step will be to work on building our coalition for the inevitable ensuing rounds of the fight. Great work with similar successes has taken place in Michigan and Washington, as well as several other states. For support and further ideas in your time of challenge, check in with ABFFE and the Media Coalition. Best of luck to all who take up the challenge of political action!

TIP LIST FOR LEGISLATIVE ACTION

• Anyone can make a difference if he or she is willing to try.

• Be prepared to make a substantial time and energy commitment.

• If you can't afford a lobbyist, work to make friends and allies in the legislature and the media. If you are working with a lobbyist not specifically in your pay, be very clear in communications with the sponsor of the lobbyist. The drawbacks of coalitions are that all parties may not be working with the exact same agenda and goals. Most lobbyists seem to prefer working quietly behind-the-scenes. Be very aware if you choose to leave the negotiations entirely in the lobbyist's hands that if he or she fails, your issue may have had minimal public exposure by your choice. This could leave you in the lurch with no time to organize. My recommendation is that you should do your own quiet campaigning for contacts, friends, and information in parallel with the lobbyist's efforts backstage. Groundwork done in that fashion could serve you very well if the lobbyist's professional strategy fails. Pressure from voters and constituents works on a very different wavelength from the lobbyist's— and sometimes it can prove more effective.

• Alliance energy helps in many ways. Coalition friends can be found in video stores, record stores, among artists and writers, and (sometimes) librarians. The different routes of communication seem to produce a clearer picture of the situation in a synergistic way. The support of friendly conversation helps keep the constructive energy rolling.

• A specific decision needs to be made about collaborating or cutting deals with the opposition. In my experience it is *not* advisable, but in some cases it may seem to be the proper course. If you are working with a coalition, you can set up a good cop/bad cop routine to apply varying pressure.

• Don't forget the resources of your local ACLU office. They came through for us when we really needed them. They are a great source of information on the political framework in your area if you are not up to speed.

CHAPTER 5

Banned Books Week

Banned Books Week offers a unique opportunity for booksellers to highlight the harms of censorship through displays and other activities. Every fall, the American Booksellers Foundation for Free Expression, the American Library Association, the American Society of Journalists and Authors, the Association of American Publishers, and the National Association of College Stores sponsor Banned Books Week. Also endorsed by the Center for the Book at the Library of Congress, this event is designed to focus attention on the First Amendment.

The American Library Association annually prepares a collection of materials to celebrate Banned Books Week. The ALA is the world's oldest and largest library association. Among its many actvities, the ALA addresses such ongoing issues as access to information, legislation and funding, intellectual freedom, and public awareness.

The theme of the week-long observance changes annually. Banned Books Week 1991 (September 28-October 5) commemorated the bicentennial of the Bill of Rights. In order to assist those participating in the event, the resource guide *Banned Books Week: Celebrating the Freedom to Read* provided posters, sample press releases, a censorship crossword puzzle, and ideas for activities and displays. This hands-on resource lists books banned the previous year and significant court cases, providing a way of tracking the censors' efforts and keeping abreast of how the courts are tackling First Amendment issues. The American Booksellers Foundation for Free

Expression distributes copies of *Banned Books Week* to ABA book store members free of charge to encourage participation in the event. The guide is also available for sale from the ALA.

Banned Books Week affords booksellers, publishers, librarians, authors, and others interested in the written word the opportunity to set aside time to concentrate on the censorship issue and send a national message. The *Banned Books Week* resource guide offers some suggestions for booksellers' participation in this annual event. The display ideas can be useful in attracting customers' attention to censorship. In addition to educating the community, an eyecatching display may reach people who would not ordinarily drop in and browse.

For more information on Banned Books Week or to obtain a copy of the resource guide, contact the American Library Association, 50 East Huron Street, Chicago, IL 60611, or the American Booksellers Foundation for Free Expression, 560 White Plains Road, Tarrytown, NY 10591.

THIRTY-FIVE BANNED BOOKS*

The following are just a sampling of titles that have been banned for a variety of reasons, ranging from using profanity, being sexually explicit, advocating a "politically incorrect" viewpoint, addressing a controversial religious issue, or even espousing a "poor philosophy of life."

1. *Adventures of Huckleberry Finn*, Mark Twain (1884).
2. *American Heritage Dictionary* (1975).
3. *And Still I Rise*, Maya Angelou (1978).

---

* The word banned is used here to indicate that the book was challenged, censored, or made unavailable in a particular locale at a particular point of time, not necessarily that all people were forbidden to read it. The dates that appear above are the original dates of publication.

4. *Another Country*, James Baldwin (1962).

5. *Black Boy*, Richard Wright (1945).

6. *Blubber*, Judy Blume (1974).

7. *Bury My Heart at Wounded Knee*, Dee Brown (1970).

8. *Carrie*, Stephen King (1974).

9. *Catch–22*, Joseph Heller (1964).

10. *Catcher in the Rye*, J.D. Salinger (1951).

11. *Charlie and the Chocolate Factory*, Roald Dahl (1976).

12. *The Chocolate War*, Robert Cormier (1974).

13. *Clan of the Cave Bear*, Jean Auel (1980).

14. *The Color Purple*, Alice Walker (1982).

15. *Death of a Salesman*, Arthur Miller (1949).

16. *The Fixer*, Bernard Malamud (1966).

17. *Flowers for Algernon*, Daniel Keyes (1966).

18. *Grapes of Wrath*, John Steinbeck (1939).

19. *The Great Gatsby*, F. Scott Fitzgerald (1925).

20. *In the Beginning: Science Faces God in the Book of Genesis*, Isaac Asimov (1981).

21. *In the Night Kitchen*, Maurice Sendak (1970).

22. *Inside the Company: CIA Diary*, Philip Agee (1974).

23. *Jaws*, Peter Benchley (1974).

24. *The Learning Tree*, Gordon Parks (1963).

25. *A Light in the Attic*, Shel Silverstein (1981).

26. *Lord of the Flies*, William Golding (1954).

27. *Oliver Twist*, Charles Dickens (1838).

28. *One Flew Over the Cuckoo's Nest*, Ken Kesey (1973).

29. *The Prince of Tides*, Pat Conroy (1986).

30. *Rules for Radicals*, Saul Alinsky (1971).

31.   *A Separate Peace*, John Knowles (1959).

32.   *Slaughterhouse–Five*, Kurt Vonnegut, Jr. (1968).

33.   *Soul on Ice*, Eldridge Cleaver (1967).

34.   *The Sun Also Rises*, Ernest Hemingway (1926).

35.   *To Kill a Mockingbird*, Harper Lee (1960).

CHAPTER 6

National Organizations Concerned with Censorship

T his list provides the names and brief descriptions of a number of organizations concerned with First Amendment rights. Working at the national level, each organization has its own particular focus, but all are working to protect the freedoms guaranteed by the First Amendment.

American Booksellers Association
Bernard E. Rath, Executive Director
560 White Plains Road
Tarrytown, New York 10591
(800) 637-0037

The American Booksellers Association (ABA) is the national trade association of the retail book industry. It has long been dedicated to defending First Amendment rights. ABA has participated in several court cases involving censorship issues, sponsored seminars and conferences to educate booksellers about their rights, and initiated Banned Books Week. In addition, a monthly magazine and weekly newsletter keep booksellers up-to-date on legislation, court cases, and other potential threats to free expression.

American Booksellers Foundation for Free Expression
Oren J. Teicher, President
560 White Plains Road
Tarrytown, NY 10591
(800) 637-0037

Launched by the American Booksellers Association at its convention in June of 1990, this not-for-profit charitable foundation has swiftly become a major force in defending First Amendment rights. The American Booksellers Foundation for Free Expression (ABFFE), in close cooperation with other organizations dedicated to preserving First Amendment rights, works to ensure the free flow of ideas and information. In addition to co-sponsoring the annual Banned Books Week activities, the Foundation publishes *Free Expression*, a quarterly newsletter that covers various censorship issues, and has sponsored major events to focus attention on protecting First Amendment rights.

American Civil Liberties Union
National Headquarters
Ira Glasser, Director
Marjorie Heins, Director, Arts Censorship Project
132 West 43rd Street
New York, NY 10036
(212) 944-9800

The American Civil Liberties Union (ACLU) is a nationwide nonpartisan organization with over 250,000 members dedicated to preserving and defending the principles embodied in the Bill of Rights. The ACLU has fifty-one state affiliates, offices in Washington, D.C., Denver, and Atlanta, and a national headquarters in New York. The Arts Censorship Project coordinates the ACLU's various activities in the fight against censorship. These include challenging legislation requiring the labeling of records and pursuing a lawsuit against the National Endowment for the Arts (NEA) regarding the so-called decency standard. Through a comprehensive program of litigation, legislation, and public education, the Arts Censorship Project focuses on issues including the right of all people to see and read uncensored books, magazines, newspapers, and art.

American Library Association
Office for Intellectual Freedom
Judith F. Krug, Executive Director
50 East Huron Street
Chicago, IL 60611
(312) 944-6780
(312) 440-9374 (fax)

Established in 1967, the American Library Association's Office for Intellectual Freedom is charged with educating librarians and the general public about the importance of intellectual freedom in libraries. Toward this goal, the office provides information and support to the library community, coordinates educational activities, and publishes the *Newsletter on Intellectual Freedom*. This bimonthly publication describes censorship incidents, summarizes recent court rulings on the First Amendment, and includes an intellectual freedom bibliography.

American Society of Journalists and Authors
Alexandra Cantor, Executive Director
1501 Broadway, Suite 302
New York, NY 10036
(212) 997-0947
(212) 768-7414 (fax)

The American Society of Journalists and Authors (ASJA) conducts an ongoing campaign against censorship under the aegis of its professional rights committee. The professional rights committee is concerned with preserving and enhancing the rights of individual writers. Since 1981, the committee has represented ASJA in the continuing fight against censorship through its annual "I Read Banned Books" campaign.

Authors' Guild

Helen Stevenson, Executive Director
Phil Stoler, Associate Director
234 West 44th Street, 10th Floor
New York, NY 10036
(212) 563-5904

The Authors' Guild is the national society of professional authors. Since its founding in 1921, it has dealt with the business and professional interests of authors. It has filed many *amicus curiae* briefs in the Supreme Court and in U.S. and state appellate courts to protect freedom of expression. Some of the many ways the Authors' Guild has been involved in the fight to protect First Amendment rights are: testimony before congressional and legislative committees; filing briefs in school book-banning cases; and the formation of a coalition with other writers' organizations that successfully lobbied to remove anti-obscenity language from 1990 legislation reauthorizing and funding the National Endowment for the Arts.

First Amendment Congress

Claudia Haskel, Executive Director
Graduate School of Public Affairs
University of Colorado at Denver
1445 Market Street, Suite 320
Denver, CO 80202
(303) 820-5688
(303) 534-8774 (fax)

The First Amendment Congress is committed to preserving freedom of expression among Americans of every persuasion by providing a continuing forum to discuss and debate the First Amendment. The congress sponsors programs such as national congresses, regional congresses, and education curriculum for grades Kindergarten through 12, as well as special reports and publications.

Freedom to Read Committee
Association of American Publishers
Betty Prashker
220 East 23rd Street
New York, NY 10010
(212) 689-8920

Affiliated with the Association of American Publishers (AAP), the Freedom to Read Committee coordinates activities to protect and strengthen First Amendment rights. The committee serves to educate the public about First Amendment issues through reports and public programs. Intervention, court cases, testimony before Congress, and coordinated action with other organizations are some of the ways the committee seeks to protect First Amendment rights.

Freedom to Read Foundation
Judith F. Krug, Executive Director
50 East Huron Street
Chicago, IL 60611
(312) 944-6780

The Freedom to Read Foundation was established in 1969 to promote and defend the right of all individuals to express their ideas without governmental interference, and to read and listen to the ideas of others. The foundation serves to nurture libraries and institutions wherein every individual's First Amendment freedoms are fulfilled. It supports the right of libraries to include in their collections and make available any work which they may legally acquire.

Freedom to Write Committee
PEN American Center
568 Broadway
New York, NY 10012
(212) 334-1660

Active both domestically and internationally, the committee protests individual instances of censorship. It acts as a member of the steering committee of the National Coalition of Writers. The coalition campaigned successfully against the controversial obscenity provision appended to National Endowment for the Arts grants. An ongoing concern of the committee is the fact that applications for NEA grants must still conform with "general standards of decency." It plans to file an *amicus curiae* brief in favor of a lawsuit challenging this new requirement.

The Freedom Writer
Skipp Porteus, National Director
P.O. Box 589
Great Barrington, MA 01230
(413) 274-3786

The Freedom Writer monitors activities that affect the First Amendment's guarantee of separation of church and state. They publish a newsletter that reports on trends and actions in court cases and society at large. Through the newsletter, the Freedom Writer hopes to alert other Americans to the way that conservative religious groups are attempting to use the legislative process to promote their views.

The Fund for Free Expression
Aryah Neier, Executive Director
488 Fifth Avenue
New York, NY 10017
(212) 972-8400

The Fund for Free Expression is the only one of the six committees of Human Rights Watch without a regional focus. The fund is concerned with freedom of expression around the world and in the United States. The fund attempts to bring a worldwide perspective to bear on American civil liberties issues and to monitor U.S. government efforts to restrict the free trade in ideas. It also prepares periodic reports on U.S. First Amendment issues, including censorship of the student press and libel suits designed to intimidate community and public interest organizations.

Media Alliance
Micah Peled, Executive Director
Fort Mason Center, Building D
San Francisco, CA 94123
(415) 441-2558

Media Alliance serves over 2,500 print and broadcast journalists and other media professionals, as well as the nonprofit community, and the general public. The alliance sponsors numerous public forums on such media issues as journalistic accountability, the First Amendment, and censorship. Recent activities include opposition to the ban on Salman Rushdie's novel, *The Satanic Verses*.

The Media Coalition, Inc.
Chris Finan, Executive Director
900 Third Avenue
New York, NY 10022
(212) 891-2070

Founded in 1973, the Media Coalition is an association that defends the First Amendment right to publish and sell books and magazines that contain some element of sexual explicitness but are not obscene under U.S. Supreme Court standards. It distributes regular reports that outline the activities of state legislatures, files legal challenges to unconstitutional laws, and files *amicus curiae* briefs in First Amendment cases involving material with sexual content.

Motion Picture Association of America
Gail Markels, Counsel
1133 Avenue of the Americas
New York, NY 10036
(212) 840-6193

The Motion Picture Association of America (MPAA) reviews all legislation at the state and local level that may impact upon the content of motion pictures, including obscenity laws, tax issues, and the ratings system. Although their primary concern is the motion picture industry, they keep close tabs on all legislation pertaining to First Amendment issues.

National Campaign for Freedom of Expression
David Mendoza, Executive Director
P.O. Box 21465
Seattle, WA 98111
(800) 477-6233

The National Campaign for Freedom of Expression (NCFE) is an educational and advocacy network of artists, art organizations, audience members, and concerned citizens formed to protect and extend freedom of artistic expression and fight censorship throughout the United States. NCFE works to empower artists in the political process at every level of public enterprise.

National Coalition Against Censorship
Leanne Katz, Executive Director
2 West 64th Street, Room 402
New York, NY 10023
(212) 724-1500

Founded in 1974, the National Coalition Against Censorship (NCAC) is the only coalition of national nonprofit organizations dedicated to fighting censorship. The coalition engages in public education and advocacy at both the national and local levels through: the dissemination of educational material; organizing conferences and public meetings; and the operation of a program to counter censorship in the schools. It also publishes a quarterly newsletter, *Censorship News*.

PEN Center USA West
Richard Bray, Executive Director
1100 Glendon Avenue, Suite 850
Los Angeles, CA 90024
(213) 824-2041

The western regional center of PEN, the international writers' organization, works on behalf of writers who have been imprisoned or censored in the Western United States and throughout the world. The center works closely with regional offices of the American Booksellers Association through special programs, including a Freedom to Write Award given to exemplary book stores.

People for the American Way
Arthur J. Kropp, President
2000 M Street NW, Suite 400
Washington, DC 20036
(202) 467-4999

Founded in 1980 by a group of civic and religious leaders, People for the American Way and its action fund have been a guiding voice devoted to our nation's heritage of tolerance and diversity. The organization provides legal, technical, and organizing assistance to communities and individuals fighting censorship. In addition, it works to: combat the intolerance of the religious right; protect women's freedom of choice; and protect and restore the civil rights of American citizens.

Video Software Dealers Association
Dan Rosenberg, Executive Vice President
3 Eves Drive, Suite 307
Marlton, NJ 08053
(609) 596-8500

The Video Software Dealers Association (VSDA) is a nonprofit international trade association with a membership exceeding 4,500 companies representing more than 25,000 retail locations. Member companies include retailers as well as manufacturers, distributors, and related businesses that constitute the home video industry. The association is active in tracking and preventing legislation designed to restrict access to constitutionally protected material, especially as it directly affects members of the home video industry. Through lobbying, the filing of briefs, and participation in lawsuits, the association maintains an important presence in the fight to protect First Amendment rights.

CHAPTER 7

Glossary

bill Legislation before it has been enacted into law.

boycott Concerted refusal to deal with another. Boycotts when used to assert a point of view (a boycott of grapes, for example, or a boycott of establishments perceived to be guilty of racism) are protected by the First Amendment. Other boycotts are generally prohibited by federal and many state anti-trust laws.

censorship Attempts by any governmental body to ban or restrict speech that is deemed dangerous or offensive. In recent years the word has been expanded to include attempts by nongovernmental groups to ban or restrict speech that they find offensive.

child pornography Sexually explicit materials using children as models. Laws criminalizing the sale or dissemination of child pornography have been enacted by Congress and by most states.

harmful to minors A term applied in minors access statutes enacted in many states, usually referring to materials that are not "obscene" as to adults but that are deemed to be harmful to minors because of their sexually explicit content.

injunction A court order requiring specified conduct to cease and desist.

LAPS A shorthand version of the third prong of the test in *Miller* v. *California*. (See *Miller* v. *California*.)

lobbying Attempting to persuade legislators to enact or not to enact specific legislation or to change or rescind existing legislation. Direct lobbying involves an attempt to educate a segment of the public regarding the merits of existing or proposed legislation, usually with a view to having the public write or call their legislators.

***Miller* v.** *California* A 1973 decision of the Supreme Court of the United States creating a three-pronged test for determining whether material was "obscene" and, therefore, not entitled to the protection of the First Amendment. Before material can be deemed obscene, it must meet *all* of the following tests:

(1) An average person, applying contemporary community standards, must find that the material applies primarily to the prurient interest.

(2) Taken as a whole, the material must be patently offensive.

(3) The material must be lacking in serious literary, artistic, political or scientific value (sometimes referred to as the LAPS test).

Minors Access Statutes Legislation that bans the production, sale or dissemination of material harmful to minors. In some cases, the legislation has been expanded to include the display of such materials in areas of an establishment where minors are likely to view them.

Minors Display Statutes Legislation seeking to prohibit the display of materials deemed harmful to minors in the window of a store, in the entrance to a theatre, or in some other place open to the public where minors are likely to view the materials.

obscenity A term applied to sexually explicit materials that are not covered by the First Amendment. (See *Miller* v. *California*.)

ordinance Legislation enacted by a municipality.

patently offensive One of the three prongs of the test set forth in *Miller* v. *California* in order to determine whether material is legally "obscene." (See *Miller* v. *California*.)

pornography Sexually explicit materials calculated to arouse lust.

prior restraint The issuance of an injunction or temporary stay order with regard to the sale, display or exhibition of materials ordinarily protected by the First Amendment (such as books, magazines, motion pictures, video tapes, musical records, etc.).

prurient appeal Calculated to arouse or heighten sexual feelings. One of the three prongs of the test set forth in *Miller* v. *California* in order to determine whether material is legally "obscene." (See *Miller* v. *California*.)

Public Nuisance Statutes A form of legislation intended to regulate or eliminate businesses or other activities deemed to constitute a public nuisance. In recent years such legislation has been applied to establishments producing or disseminating sexually explicit materials.

RICO Racketeer Influenced and Corrupt Organizations legislation. Such legislation was initially enacted by Congress in 1973 and thereafter by many states. It was originally intended to provide a weapon to police authorities with which to fight organized crime. Such legislation has gradually been expanded so that in addition to applying to what is normally perceived as organized crime, it has been redefined so as to include the sale or dissemination of two or more items which are "obscene" or "harmful to minors."

search and seizure A term used in the Fourth Amendment of the United States Constitution that bars "unreasonable searches and seizures." Where materials presumptively protected by the First Amendment are involved, the standards applied before an establishment may be searched or such materials seized are much more rigid than those applied where other materials are involved.

speech Conduct protected by the First Amendment of the United States Constitution. As interpreted by the Supreme Court, the term "speech" may include many forms of expressive conduct including symbolic actions such as wearing a black armband or burning the American flag as a means of protest.

statute State or federal legislation.

Victims Acts Laws which purport to protect and/or reimburse "victims" of certain kinds of speech. Bills and laws authorizing legal action by those who believe they were sexually assaulted as a result of pornography are presently in vogue.

This chapter was prepared by ABA counsel Max Lillienstein, of Cooperman Levitt & Winikoff, P.C., New York, NY.

CHAPTER 8

Bibliography

T he following bibliography was prepared by ABFFE Board Member Melissa Mytinger, of the Northern California Booksellers Association. It reflects only books currently in print. These sources provide an astonishing range of information about censorship and the First Amendment.

Abrashkin, William H. and Winsor, Ernest. *Freedom of Information in Massachusetts: A Practical Guide*. Westport, CT: Greenwood, 1989.

ACLU Staff and Fund for Free Expression Staff. *Free Trade in Ideas: A Conference, September 17, 1984*. Washington, DC: Center for National Security Studies, 1984.

Adler, Allan R., ed. *Litigation under the Federal Freedom of Information Act and Privacy Act: 1990*. Washington, DC: American Civil Liberties Union, 1990.

AECT Intellectual Freedom Committee. *Media, the Learner and Intellectual Freedom: A Handbook*. Washington, DC: Association for Educational Communications & Technology, 1979.

Alderfer, Hannah, et al. *Caught Looking: Feminism, Pornography & Censorship*. New York, NY: Caught Looking, Inc., 1987.

Alderman, Ellen and Kennedy, Caroline. *In Our Defense: The Bill of Rights in Action*. New York, NY: William Morrow and Company, 1991.

Alexander, James. *A Brief Narrative of the Case and Trial of John Paul Zenger, Printer of the New York Weekly Journal.* Cambridge, MA: Harvard University Press, 1972.

Allred, Stephen. *Legal Guide to Public Employee Free Speech in North Carolina.* Chapel Hill, NC: Institute of Government, 1989.

____. *The School Employee's Right of Free Speech.* Chapel Hill, NC: Institute of Government, 1989.

Altschull, J. Herbert. *From Milton to McLuhan: The Ideas Behind American Journalism.* White Plains, NY: Longman Publishing Group, 1990.

Amundson, Kristen. *Challenges for School Leaders.* Arlington, VA: American Association of School Administrators, 1988.

Anastaplo, George. *The Constitutionalist: Notes on the First Amendment.* Ann Arbor, MI: Books on Demand, 1971.

Anderson, Arthur J. *Problems in Intellectual Freedom and Censorship.* Ann Arbor, MI: Books on Demand, 1974.

Anderson, Douglas A. *Washington Merry-Go-Round of Libel Actions.* Chicago, IL: Nelson-Hall, 1980.

Association of Legal and Social Philosophy. *Freedom of Speech: Basis and Limits.* Philadelphia, PA: Coronet Books, 1986.

Auerbach, Jerold S. *Labor and Liberty: The La Follette Committee and the New Deal.* New York, NY: Irvington Publishers, 1966.

Backes, James G. and Shields, Donald J. *History of Free Speech in Decision Making.* Dubuque, IA: Kendall Hunt Publishing Company, 1985.

Baker, C. Edwin. *Human Liberty and Freedom of Speech.* New York, NY: Oxford University Press, Inc., 1989.

Ball, W. Valentine. *The Law of Libel as Affecting Newspapers and Journalists.* Littleton, CO: Fred B. Rothman & Company, 1986.

Barendt, Eric. *Freedom of Speech*. New York, NY: Oxford University Press, Inc., 1987.

Barron, Jerome A. *Freedom of the Press for Whom?: The Right of Access to Mass Media*. Ann Arbor, MI: Books on Demand, 1973.

Bartlett, Jonathan, ed. *The First Amendment in a Free Society*. New York, NY: H.W. Wilson, 1979.

Beasley, Maurine and Gibbons, Sheila. *Women in Media: A Documentary Source Book*. Washington, DC: Women's Institute for the Freedom of the Press, 1977.

Beman, Lamar T., ed. *Selected Articles on Censorship of Speech and the Press*. New York, NY: AMS Press, 1969.

Berninghausen, David K. *The Flight from Reason: Essays on Intellectual Freedom in the Academy, the Press, and the Library*. Chicago, IL: American Library Association, 1975.

Berns, Walter. *The First Amendment and the Future of American Democracy*. Washington, DC: Regnery Gateway Inc., 1976.

_____. *Freedom, Virtue and the First Amendment*. Westport, CT: Greenwood Publishing Group, Inc., 1957.

Bezanson, Randall P., et al. *Libel Law and the Press: Myth and Reality*. New York, NY: Free Press, 1987.

Bhattacharya, Hiranmoy. *Raj and Literature: Banned Begali Books*. Columbia, MO: South Asia Books, 1989.

Birkinshaw, Patrick. *Freedom of Information: The Law, the Practice and the Ideal*. Littleton, CO: Rothman & Company, 1988.

Blanchard, Margaret A. *Exporting the First Amendment: The Press Government Crusade of 1945-1952*. New York, NY: Longman, 1986.

Blue, Martha. *By the Book: Legal ABC's for the Printed Word*. Flagstaff, AZ: Northland Publishing, 1990.

Bollan, William. *The Freedom of Speech and Writing upon Public Affairs Considered.* Civil Liberties in American History Series. New York, NY: Da Capo Press, Inc., 1970.

Bollinger, Lee C. *The Tolerant Society.* New York, NY: Oxford University Press, Inc., 1988.

Bosmajian, Haig, ed. *The Freedom of Expression.* New York, NY: Neal-Schuman Publishers, 1988.

____, ed. *The Freedom to Publish.* New York, NY: Neal-Schuman Publishers, 1989.

____, ed. *The Freedom to Read.* New York, NY: Neal-Schuman Publishers, 1987.

____. *Justice Douglas and Freedom of Speech.* Metuchen, NJ: Scarecrow Press, 1980.

____. *The Principles and Practices of Freedom of Speech.* Lanham, MD: University Press of America, 1983.

Boyle, Kevin, ed. *Article Nineteen World Report 1988: Information, Freedom & Censorship.* New York, NY: Times Books, 1988.

Brady, John F., ed. *Community Right to Know Compliance Handbook.* Madison, CT: Business and Legal Reports, 1988.

____. ed. *The Supervisor's Right to Know Handbook.* Madison, CT: Business and Legal Reports, 1988.

Braveman, Burt A. and Chetwynd, Frances J. *Information Law: Freedom of Information, Privacy, Open Meetings, Other Access Laws.* New York, NY: Practising Law Institute, 1986.

Brownmiller, Susan. *Against Our Will: Men, Women and Rape.* New York, NY: Simon & Schuster, 1975.

Bryan, T. Avril. *Censorship and the Social Conflict in the Spanish Theatre: The Case of Alfonso Sastre.* Washington, DC: University Press of America, 1983.

Burress, Lee. *Battle of the Books: Literary Censorship in the Public Schools, 1950-1985.* Metuchen, NJ: Scarecrow Press, 1989.

Burstyn, Varda, ed. *Women Against Censorship*. Vancouver, BC: Salem House, 1985.

Canavan, Francis. *Freedom of Expression: Purpose as Limit*. Durham, NC: Carolina Academy Press, and Claremont Institute for the Study of Statesmanship and Political Philosophy, 1984.

Carlson, Julia, ed. *Banned in Ireland: Censorship and the Irish Writer*. Athens, GA: University of Georgia Press, 1990.

Carmilly, Moshe. *Fear of Art*. New York, NY: R.R. Bowker, 1986.

Carter-Ruck, Peter. *Libel and Slander*. Hamden, CT: Shoestring Press, Inc., 1973.

Casper, Dale E. *The Freedom of Information Act: Journal Articles, 1982-1988*. Monticello, IL: Vance Bibliographies, 1989.

Chadwick, Owen. *Catholicism and History: The Opening of the Vatican Archives*. New York, NY: Cambridge University Press, 1978.

Chafee, Zechariah. *The Inquiring Mind*. Reprint of 1928 edition. New York, NY: Da Capo Press, Inc., 1974.

Chanin, Abraham S. *The Flames of Freedom*. Lanham, MD: University Press of America, 1990.

Chevigny, Paul. *More Speech: Dialogue Rights and Modern Liberty*. Philadelphia, PA: Temple University Press, 1988.

Choldin, Marianna T. *A Fence Around the Empire: Russian Censorship of Western Ideas under the Tsars*. Durham, NC: Duke University Press, 1985.

_____ and Friedberg, Maurice. *The Red Pencil: Artists, Scholars and Censors in the U.S.S.R.* Boston, MA: Unwin Hyman, 1989.

Citizens Guide on How to Use the Freedom of Information Act and the Privacy Act Requesting Government Documents. Brooklyn, NY: Revisionist Press, 1984.

Claflin, Stephen T., Jr. A Radical Proposal for Full Use of Free Speech. New York, NY: Philosophical Library Inc., 1979.

Clearinghouse on School Book-Banning Litigation Staff. *Books on Trial.* New York, NY: National Coalition Against Censorship, 1985.

Clor, Harry M. *Obscenity and Public Morality: Censorship in a Liberal Society.* Chicago, IL: University of Chicago Press, 1985.

Clyde, William M. *Struggle for the Freedom of the Press from Caxton to Cromwell.* Reprint of 1934 edition. New York, NY: Burt Franklin Publisher, 1970.

Cobbett, William. *Democratic Judge Or, the Equal Liberty of the Press.* Reprint of 1798 edition. Salem, NH: Ayer Company Publishers, Inc., 1970.

Cohen, Jeremy. *Congress Shall Make No Law: Oliver Wendell Holmes, the First Amendment and Judicial Decision-Making.* Ames, IA: Iowa State University Press, 1989.

Cohen, Ruth. *Whose File Is It Anyway.* New York, NY: State Mutual Book and Periodical Service, Ltd., 1988.

Cohn-Sherbok, Dan., ed. *The Salman Rushdie Controversy in Inter-Religious Perspective.* Lewiston, TX: E. Mellen Press, 1990.

Conference on Intellectual Freedom, 1965, Washington, DC. *Freedom of Inquiry: Supporting the Library Bill of Rights.* Reprint of 1965 edition. Ann Arbor, MI: Books on Demand, 1982.

Conquest, Robert. *Tyrants and Typewriters: Communiques from the Struggle for Truth.* Lexington, VA: Lexington Books, 1989.

The Consequences of "Pre-Publication Review:" A Case Study of CIA Censorship of 'The CIA and the Cult of Intelligence.' Washington, DC: The Center for National Security Studies, 1983.

Cook, Philip S., ed. *Liberty of Expression*. Washington, DC: Wilson Center Press, 1990.

Cooper, R. John and Sanford, Bruce W. *First Amendment and Libel: The Experts Look at Print, Broadcast and Cable*. Orlando, FL: Harcourt Brace Jovanovich, Inc.

Cooper, Thomas. *Treatise on the Law of Libel and the Liberty of the Press*. Civil Liberties in American History Series. New York, NY: Da Capo Press, Inc., 1970.

Copp, David and Wendell, Susan, eds. *Pornography and Censorship*. Buffalo, NY: Prometheus Books, 1982.

Cornwell, Roger and Staunton, Marie. *Data Protection: Putting the Record Straight*. New York, NY: State Mutual Book and Periodical Service, Ltd., 1988.

Cox, Archibald. *The Court and the Constitution*. Boston, MA: Houghton Mifflin, 1987.

_____. *Freedom of Expression*. Cambridge, MA: Harvard University Press, 1981.

Cox, C. Benjamin. The Censorship Game and How to Play It. Arlington, VA: National Council for the Social Studies, 1977.

Craig, Alec. The Banned Books of England and Other Countries: A Study of the Conception of Literary Obscenity. Reprint of the 1962 edition. Westport, CT: Greenwood Publishing Group, Inc., 1977.

Cross, Harold L. *People's Right to Know*. New York, NY: AMS Press, Inc., 1953.

Csorba, Les, III., ed. *Academic License: The War on Academic Freedom*. Evanston, IL: United Communications of America, Inc., 1988.

Curry, Jane L. *Press Control Around the World*. New York, NY: Praeger Publishers, 1982.

Curry, Richard O., ed. *Freedom at Risk: Secrecy, Censorship, & Repression in the 1980's*. Philadelphia, PA: Temple University Press, 1988.

Daily, Jay E. *The Anatomy of Censorship*. New York, NY: Marcel Dekker, Inc., 1973.

Davidson, Roger and White, Phil, eds. *Information and Government: Studies in the Dynamics of Policy-Making*. Edinburgh, Scotland: Edinburgh University Press, 1988.

Davis, James E., ed. *Dealing with Censorship*. Urbana, IL: National Council of Teachers of English, 1979.

Dawson, Samuel A. *Freedom of the Press: A Study of the Legal Doctrine of 'Qualified Privilege.'* Littleton, CO: Rothman & Company, 1982.

Demac, Donna A. *Liberty Denied: The Current Rise of Censorship in America*. New Brunswick, NJ: Rutgers University Press, 1990.

Dennis, Everette E., et al., eds. *Media Freedom and Accountability*. New York, NY: Greenwood Press, 1989.

Devol, Kenneth S. Mass Media and the Supreme Court. 4th edition. Mamaroneck, NY: Hastings House Publishers, 1990.

Dickerson, Donna L. *Freedom of the Press in Nineteenth-Century America*. New York, NY: Greenwood Press, 1990.

Dill, Barbara. *The Journalist's Handbook on Libel and Privacy*. New York, NY: Free Press, 1986.

Ditchfield, Peter H. *Books Fatal to Their Authors*. Reprint of 1895 edition. New York, NY: Burt Franklin, Publisher, 1970.

Donnerstein, Edward, et al. *The Question of Pornography: Research Findings and Policy Implications*. New York, NY: Free Press, 1987.

Downs, Robert B. and McCoy, Ralph E., eds. *The First Freedom Today: Critical Issues Relating to Censorship and to Intellectual Freedom*. Chicago, IL: American Library Association, 1984.

DuBoff, Leonard D. *Book Publishers' Legal Guide*. Salem, NH: Butterworths U.S., Legal Publishers, Inc., 1984.

Dunayevskaya, Raya, Savio, Mario and Walker, Eugene. *The Free Speech Movement and the Negro Revolution.* Chicago, IL: News and Letters Committees, 1965.

Duniway, Clyde A. *The Development of Freedom of the Press in Massachusetts.* Reprint of 1906 edition. New York, NY: Burt Franklin, Publisher, 1969.

Dworkin, Andrea. *Pornography: Men Possessing Women.* New York, NY: Putnam, 1981.

_____ and MacKinnon, Catharine A. *Pornography and Civil Rights: A New Day for Women's Equality.* Minneapolis, MN: Organizing Against Pornography, 1988.

Education and Labor Committee. *Violations of Free Speech and Rights of Labor: Proceedings of the Committee on Education and Labor, U.S. Senate, 76th Congress, 3rd Session.* Reprint of 1941 edition. Salem, NH: Ayer Company Publishers, Inc., 1975.

Elder, David A. *The Fair Report Privilege.* Salem, NH: Butterworths U.S., Legal Publishers, Inc., 1988.

Entertainment, Publishing, and Sports Law. New Providence, NJ: R. R. Bowker, 1989.

Ernst, M.L. *The First Freedom.* Reprint of 1946 edition. New York, NY: Da Capo Press, Inc., 1971.

_____ and Seagle, W. *To the Pure: A Study of Obscenity and the Censor.* Reprint of 1928 edition. Millwood, NY: Kraus Reprint and Periodicals.

Feiffer, Jules, Kimmel, Michael and Masson, Jeffrey, eds. *Men Confront Pornography.* New York, NY: Crown Publishers, Inc., 1990.

Ferlinghetti, Lawrence and Ehrlich, J.W., eds. *Howl of the Censor: Lawrence Ferlinghetti, Defendant.* Reprint of 1961 edition. San Carlos, CA: Nourse Publishing Company, 1976.

The First Amendment and Libel Litigation. Harrisburg, PA: Pennsylvania Bar Institute, 1987.

The First Five-Year Annotated Index to Media Report to Women: 1972-1976. Washington, DC: Women's Institute for Freedom of the Press, 1977.

Fisk, Theophilus. *Orations on the Freedom of the Press.* Reprint of 1837 edition. Salem, NH: Ayer Company Publishers, Inc., 1970.

Forer, Lois G. *A Chilling Effect: The Mounting Threat of Libel and Invasion of Privacy Actions to the First Amendment.* New York, NY: W.W. Norton and Company, 1987.

Fortenberry, Ken H. *Kill the Messenger: One Man's Fight Against Bigotry and Greed.* Atlanta, GA: Peachtree Publishers, 1989.

Francois, William E. *Mass Media Law and Regulation.* Columbus, OH: Grid, Inc., 1978.

Franklin, Benjamin. *An Apology for Printers.* New York, NY: Book Craftsmen Associates, 1955.

Freedman, Warren. *Freedom of Speech on Private Property.* New York, NY: Quorum Books, 1988.

Friendly, Fred W. *Minnesota Rag.* New York, NY: Random House, Inc., 1982.

From Official Files: Abstracts of Documents on National Security and Civil Liberties Available from the Center for National Security Studies Library. Washington, DC: Center for National Security Studies, 1985.

Gartner, Michael G. *Advertising and the First Amendment.* New York, NY: Priority Press Publications/Twentieth Century Fund, 1989.

Geller, Evelyn. *Forbidden Books in American Public Libraries, 1876-1939: A Study in Cultural Change.* Westport, CT: Greenwood Publishing Group, 1984.

Georgetown Law Journal Editors. *Georgetown Law Journal: Media & the First Amendment in a Free Society.* Amherst, MA: University of Massachusetts Press, 1973.

Georgiady, Nicholas P. and Romano, Louis G. *Focus on Censorship & the Middle School.* East Lansing, MI: Michigan Association of Middle School Educators.

Gerber, Albert B. *Sex, Pornography and Justice.* New York, NY: L. Stuart, 1965.

Gibson, James L. and Bingham, Richard D. *Civil Liberties and Nazis: The Skokie Free-Speech Controversy.* New York, NY: Praeger Publishers, 1985.

Gillmor, Donald M. and Barron, Jerome A. *Mass Communication Law.* St. Paul, MN: West Publishing Company, 1979.

Goldstein, Michael J., Kant, Harold S., and Hartman, John J. *Pornography & Sexual Deviance.* Berkeley, CA: University of California Press, 1973.

Goldstein, Robert J. *Censorship of Political Caricature in Nineteenth-Century France.* Kent, OH: Kent State University Press, 1989.

_____. *Political Censorship of the Arts and the Press in Nineteenth-Century Europe.* New York, NY: St. Martin's Press, 1989.

Gonzalez Faus, Jose I. *Where the Spirit Breathes Prophetic Dissent in the Church.* Maryknoll, NY: Orbis Books, 1988.

Goodale, James C., ed. *The New York Times Co. vs. U.S.: Pentagon Papers Litigation.* Salem, NH: Ayer Company Publishers, Inc., 1971.

Goodman, Michael B. *Contemporary Literary Censorship: The Case History of Burroughs' Naked Lunch.* Metuchen, NJ: Scarecrow Press, Inc., 1981.

Gordon, Andrew C. and Heinz, John P., eds. *Public Access to Information.* New Brunswick, NJ: Transaction Books, 1979.

Gordon, George N. *Erotic Communications: Studies in Sex, Sin and Censorship.* Hastings, NY: Hastings House, 1980.

Green, Jonathon. *The Encyclopedia of Censorship.* New York, NY: Facts on File, Inc., 1990.

Greenawalt, Kent. *Speech, Crime, and the Uses of Language.* New York, NY: Oxford University Press, Inc., 1989.

Griffin, Susan. *Pornography and Silence.* New York, NY: Harper & Row, 1981.

Hachten, William and Giffard, C. Anthony. *The Press and Apartheid: Repression and Propaganda in South Africa.* Madison, WI: University of Wisconsin Press, 1984.

Haiman, Franklyn S. *Speech and Law in a Free Society.* Chicago, IL: University of Chicago Press, 1981.

Hand, Learned. *The Bill of Rights.* New York, NY: Macmillan Publishing Company, Inc., 1964.

Haney, Robert W. *Comstockery in America: Patterns of Censorship and Control.* Reprint of 1960 edition. New York, NY: Da Capo Press, Inc., 1974.

Harig, Katherine J. *Libraries, the Military and Civilian Life.* Hamden, CT: Library Professional Publications, 1989.

Hart, William H. *Index Expurgatorius Angelicanus, Catalogue of Books Suppressed or Burnt by the Common Hangman, 1523-1681.* Reprint of 1878 edition. New York, NY: Burt Franklin, Publisher, 1969.

Hay, George. *Essay on the Liberty of the Press.* Reprint of 1799 edition. Salem, NH: Ayer Company Publishers, Inc., 1970.

____. *Two Essays on the Liberty of the Press.* Reprint of 1803 edition. New York, NY: Da Capo Press, Inc., 1970.

Hemmer, Joseph J., Jr. *The Supreme Court and the First Amendment.* Westport, CT: Greenwood Publishing Group, 1986.

Hentoff, Nat. *The First Freedom: The Tumultuous History of Free Speech in America.* New York, NY: Delacorte Press, 1980.

Hernon, Peter and McClure, Charles R. *Federal Information Policies in the 1980's: Conflicts and Issues.* Norwood, CT: Ablex Publishing Corporation, 1987.

Higman, F. *Censorship and the Sorbonne.* Geneve, Suisse: Druz, 1979.

Hocking, William E. *Freedom of the Press.* Reprint of 1947 edition. New York, NY: Da Capo Press, Inc., 1972.

Hoffman, Frank. *Intellectual Freedom and Censorship: An Annotated Bibliography.* Metuchen, NJ: Scarecrow Press, Inc., 1987.

Holmes, Deborah. *Governing the Press: Limitations on Media Freedom in the United States and Great Britain.* Boulder, CO: Westview Press, 1986.

Hull, Elizabeth. *Taking Liberties: National Barriers to the Free Flow of Ideas.* New York, NY: Praeger Publishers, 1990.

Hurwitz, Leon. *Historical Dictionary of Censorship in the United States.* Westport, CT: Greenwood Publishing Group, 1985.

Ide, Arthur F. *Evangelical Terrorism: Censorship, Jerry Falwell, Pat Robertson and the Seamy Side of Christian Fundamentalism.* Irving, TX: Scholars Books, 1986.

Ingelhart, Louis E. *Press Freedoms: A Descriptive Calendar of Concepts, Interpretations, Events and Court Actions, from 4000 BC to the Present.* Westport, CT: Greenwood Publishing Group, Inc., 1987.

____. *Press Law and Press Freedom for High School Publications: Court Cases and Related Decisions Discussing Free Expression Guarantees and Limitations for High School Students and Journalists.* Westport, CT: Greenwood Publishing Group, Inc., 1986.

Jackson, Holbrook. *The Fear of Books.* Reprint of 1932 edition. Westport, CT: Greenwood Publishing Group, Inc., 1982.

Jacobson, Helen S., ed. *The Diary of a Russian Censor: Aleksandr Nikitenko.* Amherst, MA: University of Massachusetts Press, 1975.

Jansen, Sue C. *Censorship: The Knot That Binds Power and Knowledge.* New York, NY: Oxford University Press, Inc., 1988.

Jenson, Carol E. *The Network of Control: State Supreme Courts and State Security Statutes, 1920-1970.* Westport, CT: Greenwood Publishing Group, Inc., 1982.

Kahn, Albert. *The Matusow Affair: Memoir of a National Scandal.* Mt. Kisco, NY: Moyer Bell Ltd., 1987.

Kalven, Harry, Jr. *Negro and the First Amendment.* Chicago, IL: University of Chicago Press, 1966.

____. *A Worthy Tradition: Freedom of Speech in America.* New York, NY: Harper and Row, 1988.

Kane, Peter E. *Murder, Courts and the Press: Issues in Free Press Fair Trial.* Carbondale, IL: Southern Illinois University Press, 1986.

Kaplan, Craig and Schrecker, Ellen, eds. *Regulating the Intellectuals: Perspectives on Academic Freedom in the 1980's.* New York, NY: Praeger Publishers, 1983.

Kelly, Sean. *Access Denied: The Politics of Censorship.* Lanham, MD: University Press of America, 1978.

Kessler, Lauren. *The Dissident Press.* Beverly Hills, CA: Sage Publications, 1984.

Kilpatrick, James J. *The Smut Peddlers.* Reprint of 1960 edition. Westport, CT: Greenwood Publishing Group, Inc., 1973.

King, Jerome B. *Law v. Order: Legal Process and Free Speech in Contemporary France.* Hamden, CT: Shoe String Press, Inc., 1975.

Kronhausen, Eberhard and Phyllis. *Pornography and the Law: The Psychology of Erotic Realism and Pornography.* New York, NY: Ballantine Books, 1964.

Kupferman, Theodore, ed. *Censorship, Secrecy, Access, and Obscenity: Readings from Communications and the Law*, Vol. 3. Westport, CT: Meckler Corporation, 1990.

Kurland, Philip B. *Free Speech and Association: The Supreme Court and the First Amendment*. Westport, CT: Meckler Corporation, 1990.

Labunski, Richard. *Libel and the First Amendment: Legal History and Practice in Print and Broadcasting*. New Brunswick, NJ: Transaction Books, 1987.

Lacy, Dan M. *Freedom and Communications*. Champaign, IL: University of Illinois Press, 1965.

Lederer, Laura., ed. *Take Back the Night: Women on Pornography*. New York, NY: Morrow, 1980.

Leigh, Robert D. *A Free and Responsible Press, a General Report on Mass Communication: Newspapers, Radio, Motion Pictures, Magazines and Books*. Chicago, IL: University of Chicago Press, 1974.

Lewis, Anthony. *Make No Law: The Sullivan Case and the First Amendment*. New York, NY: Random House, 1991.

Lewis, Felice F. *Literature, Obscenity, and Law*. Carbondale, IL: Southern Illinois University Press, 1978.

Lewis, Wyndham. *The Writer and the Absolute*. Reprint of 1952 edition. New York, NY: Greenwood Press, 1975.

Lichtenberg, Judith. *Democracy and the Mass Media*. New York, NY: Cambridge University Press, 1990.

____. Foundations and Limits of Freedom of the Press. College Park, MD: Institute for Philosophy and Public Policy, 1987.

Lillico, Joris. *Freedom Handbook*. Cedar City, UT: Ralston-Pilot Inc., Publishers, 1978.

Littlewood, Thomas B. *Coals of Fire: The "Alton Telegraph" Libel Case*. Carbondale, IL: Southern Illinois University Press, 1988.

Lofton, John. *The Press as Guardian of the First Amendment*. Columbia, SC: University of South Carolina, 1980.

Lowry, George G. and Lowry, Robert C. *Lowrys' Handbook of Right-to-Know and Emergency Planning*. Chelsea, MI: Lewis Publishers, 1988.

Lynn, Barry. *Polluting the Censorship Debate: A Summary and Critique of the Final Report of the Attorney General's Commission on Pornography.* Washington, DC: American Civil Liberties Union, 1986.

MacKinnon, Catharine A. *Feminism Unmodified: Discourses on Life and Law.* Cambridge, MA: Harvard University Press, 1987.

McCarthy, Eugene J. *The Ultimate Tyranny: The Majority over the Majority.* New York, NY: Harcourt Brace Jovanovich, Inc., 1980.

McClure, Charles R., et al. *United States Government Information Policies: Views and Perspectives.* Norwood, CT: Ablex Publishing Corporation, 1989.

McCormick, Robert. *Freedom of the Press.* Reprint of 1936 edition. Salem, NH: Ayer Company Publishers, 1970.

McCoy, Ralph E. *Freedom of the Press: An Annotated Bibliography.* Carbondale, IL: Southern Illinois University Press, 1968.

____. *Freedom of the Press: A Bibliocyclopedia. Ten Year Supplement (1967-1977).* Carbondale, IL: Southern Illinois University Press, 1979.

Macur, Mary. *Curious What You Might Find When You Go Out to Look for Elephants.* Mill Valley, CA: First Amendment Press.

Maitland, Sara and Appignanesi, Lisa, eds. *The Rushdie File.* Syracuse, NY: Syracuse University Press, 1990.

Marsh, Dave. *50 Ways to Fight Censorship.* New York, NY: Thunder's Mouth Press, 1991.

Marwick, Christine M. *Your Right to Government Information.* Carbondale, IL: Southern Illinois University Press, 1985.

Meese Commission Exposed: Proceedings of a National Coalition Against Censorship Public Information Briefing on the Attorney General's Commission on Pornography. New York, NY: National Coalition Against Censorship, 1987.

Mehra, Achal. *Free Flow of Information: A New Paradigm.* Westport, CT: Greenwood Publishing Group, 1986.

Meiklejohn, Alexander. *Political Freedom: The Constitutional Powers of the People.* Reprint of 1960 edition. Westport, CT: Greenwood Publishing Group, Inc., 1979.

Mencken, H.L. *The Editor, the Bluenose, and the Prostitute: H.L. Mencken's History of the "Hatrack" Censorship Case.* Boulder, CO: Roberts Rinehart, 1988.

Merrill, John C. *The Dialectic in Journalism: Toward a Responsible Use of Press Freedom.* Baton Rouge, LA: Louisiana State University Press, 1989.

Mickelson, Sig and Teran, Elena M., eds. *The First Amendment—The Challenge of New Technology.* New York, NY: Praeger Publishers, 1989.

Middleton, Kent and Chamberlin, Bill F. *The Law of Public Communication.* White Plains, NY: Longman Publishing Group, 1991.

Mill, James. *Essays on Government, Jurisprudence, Liberty of the Press and Law of Nations, Reprinted from the Supplement to the Encyclopaedia Britannica.* Reprint of 1825 edition. New York, NY: Augustus M. Kelley Publishers, 1986.

Mill, John Stuart. *On Liberty: Freedom of Speech.* Reprint of 1874 edition. Stockton, CA: Becoming-One Publications, 1990.

Mitchell, Richard H. *Censorship in Imperial Japan.* Princeton, NJ: Princeton University Press, 1983.

Monroe, Judy. *Censorship.* Riverside, NJ: Crestwood House, 1990.

Morales, Cecilio J., Jr., et al., eds. *A Survey of Press Freedom in Latin America 1985-1986.* Washington, DC: Council on Hemispheric Affairs, 1986.

Moretti, Daniel S. *Obscenity and Pornography: The Law under the First Amendment.* Dobbs Ferry, NY: Oceana Publications, Inc., 1984.

Morgan, George A. *Speech & Society: The Christian Linguistic Social Philosophy of Eugene Rosenstock-Huessy.* Gainesville, FL: University Presses of Florida, 1987.

Moshman, David. *Children, Education, and the First Amendment: A Psycholegal Analysis.* Lincoln, NB: University of Nebraska Press, 1989.

_____, ed. *Free Press.* The Bill of Rights & American Legal History Series. New York, NY: Garland Publishing, Inc., 1990.

Murphy, Paul. *The Meaning of Freedom of Speech.* Westport, CT: Greenwood Publishing Group, 1972.

National Association of Broadcasters Staff. *Broadcasting and the Bill of Rights: Statements on the White Bill.* Reprint of 1947 edition. New York, NY: Burt Franklin Publisher, 1972.

National Issues Forum Staff. *Freedom of Speech: Where to Draw the Line.* Dubuque, IA: Kendall-Hunt Publishing Company, 1989.

Nelson, Harold N., ed. *Freedom of the Press from Hamilton to the Warren Court.* New York, NY: Macmillan Publishing Company, Inc., 1967.

Nelson, Jack and Roberts, Gene, Jr. *The Censors and the Schools.* Reprint of 1963 edition. Westport, CT: Greenwood Publishing Company, Inc., 1977.

New York Public Library Staff. *Censorship: Five Hundred Years of Conflict.* New York, NY: Oxford University Press, Inc., 1984.

Newman, Jay. *The Journalist in Plato's Cave.* Rutherford, NJ: Fairleigh Dickinson University, 1989.

Niczow, Aleksandar. *Black Book of Polish Censorship.* South Bend, IN: And Books, 1982.

Noble, William. *Bookbanning in America: Who Bans Books and Why.* Middlebury, VT: P.S. Eriksson, 1990.

Nordquist, Joan, ed. *Pornography and Censorship.* Santa Cruz, CA: Reference and Research Services, 1987.

Norwick, Kenneth P., ed. *Lobbying for Freedom in the 1980's: A Grassroots Guide to Protecting Your Rights*. New York, NY: Perigree Books, 1983.

Oboler, Eli. *Defending Intellectual Freedom: The Library and the Censor*. Westport, CT: Greenwood Publishing Group, Inc., 1980.

____. *The Fear of the Word: Censorship and Sex*. Metuchen, NJ: Scarecrow Press, Inc., 1974.

O'Brien, David M. *The Public's Right to Know: The Supreme Court and the First Amendment*. New York, NY: Praeger Publishers, 1981.

O'Neil, Robert M. *Free Speech: Responsible Communication under Law*. New York, NY: Macmillan Publishing Company, Inc., 1972.

O'Reilly, James T. *Federal Information Disclosure: Procedures, Forms and the Law*. Colorado Springs, CO: Shepard's/McGraw-Hill, Inc., 1977.

Orloff, Neil and Sakai, Susan. *Community Right-to-Know Handbook: A Guide to Compliance with the Emergency Planning and Community Right-to-Know Act*. New York, NY: Clark Boardman Company, Ltd., 1988.

Orr, Lisa, ed. *Censorship: Opposing Viewpoints*. San Diego, CA: Greenhaven Press, 1990.

Overbeck, Wayne and Pullen, Rick D. *Major Principles of Media Law*. Fort Worth, TX: Holt Rinehart and Winston, Inc., 1985.

Packer, Cathy. *Freedom of Expression in the American Military: A Communication Modeling Analysis*. New York, NY: Praeger Publishers, 1989.

Parsons, Patrick. *Cable Television and the First Amendment*. Lexington, KY: Lexington Books, 1987.

Paterson, James. *The Liberty of the Press, Speech, and Public Worship: Being Commentaries on the Liberty of the Subject and the Laws of England.* Reprint of 1880 edition. Littleton, CO: Rothman & Company, 1985.

Patterson, Annabel M. *Censorship and Interpretation: The Conditions of Writing and Reading in Early Modern England.* Madison, WI: University of Wisconsin Press, 1990.

Paul, James C. and Schwartz, Murray L. *Federal Censorship: Obscenity in the Mail.* Reprint of 1961 edition. Westport, CT: Greenwood Publishing Group, Inc., 1977.

Peattie, Noel. *A Passage for Dissent: The Best of Sipapu, 1970-1988.* Jefferson, NC: McFarland and Company, 1989.

Peck, Robert S. and Manemann, Mary. *Speaking and Writing Truth: Community Forums on the First Amendment.* Chicago, IL: American Bar Association, 1985.

Pederson, Marguerite. *Censorship in the U.S.* Rochester, WA: Sovereign Press, 1986.

Pell, Eve. *The Big Chill: New Dangers to Free Speech in America.* Boston, MA: Beacon, 1984.

Ploman, Edward W., ed. *International Law Governing Communications and Information: A Collection of Documents.* Westport, CT: Greenwood Publishing Group, Inc., 1982.

Polenberg, Richard. *Fighting Faiths: The Abrams Case, the Supreme Court and Free Speech.* New York, NY: Viking Penguin, 1989.

Popper, William. *Censorship of Hebrew Books.* Reprint of 1899 edition. New York, NY: Burt Franklin, Publisher.

Putnam, George H. *Censorship of the Church of Rome and Its Influence upon the Production and Distribution of Literature.* Reprint of 1906 edition. Salem, NH: Ayer Company Publishers, Inc., 1967.

Reichman, Henry F. *Censorship and Selection: Issues and Answers for Schools.* Arlington, VA: American Library Association, 1988.

Rembar, Charles. *The End of Obscenity: The Trials of Lady Chatterley, Tropic of Cancer, and Fanny Hill.* New York, NY: Harper and Row, 1986.

Ripoll, Carlos. *The Heresy of Words in Cuba*. New York, NY: Freedom House, 1985.

Rips, Geoffrey. *Un–American Activities: The Campaign Against the Underground Press*. San Francisco, CA: City Lights Books, 1981.

Robertson, Geoffrey. *Obscenity: An Account of Censorship Laws and Their Enforcement in England and Wales*. Littleton, CO: Rothman & Company, 1979.

Rodgers, Raymond S., ed. *Free Speech Yearbook: 1990*. Carbondale, IL: Southern Illinois University Press, 1991.

Rogers, Denise, ed. *Selected Bibliography of Books and Articles on Censorship (1950-1983)*. St. Louis, MO: Washington University School of Law Library, 1983.

Rogers, Donald J. *Banned! Book Censorship in the Schools*. New York, NY: Messner, 1987.

Rogge, O. John. *First and the Fifth*. Reprint of 1960 edition. New York, NY: Da Capo Press, Inc., 1971.

Rome, Edwin P. and Roberts, William H. *Corporate and Commercial Free Speech: First Amendment Protection of Expression in Business*. Westport, CT: Quorum Books, 1985.

Rose, Arnold M. *Libel and Academic Freedom: A Lawsuit Against Political Extremists*. Reprint of 1968 edition. Ann Arbor, MI: Books on Demand.

Rucker, Bryce W. *First Freedom*. Carbondale, IL: Southern Illinois University Press, 1968.

Russell, Diana. *Sexual Exploitation: Rape, Child Sexual Abuse and Workplace Harassment*. Beverly Hills, CA: Sage Publications, 1984.

Rutherford, Livingston and Bell, James B. John Peter Zenger and Freedom of the Press. Mount Vernon, NY: A. Colish Inc.

Rutland, Robert Allen. *The Birth of the Bill of Rights 1776-1791*. New York, NY: Collier Books, 1962.

St. John-Stevas, Norman. *Obscenity and the Law*. Reprint of 1956 edition. New York, NY: Da Capo Press, Inc., 1974.

Schauer, Frederick. *Free Speech: A Philosophical Enquiry*. New York, NY: Cambridge University Press, 1982.

Schexnaydre, Linda and Burns, Nancy. *Censorship: A Guide for Successful Workshop Planning*. Phoenix, AZ: Oryx Press, 1984.

Schlesinger, Philip and Griffith, John. *Free Speech for All?* New York, NY: State Mutual Book and Periodical Service, Ltd., 1979.

Schopflin, George. *Censorship and Political Communication in Eastern Europe: A Collection of Documents*. New York, NY: St. Martin's Press, 1983.

Schroeder, Theodore A. *Constitutional Free Speech Defined and Defended*. Reprint of 1919 edition. New York, NY: Da Capo Press, Inc., 1970.

____. *Free Press Anthology*. Reprint of 1909 edition. Littleton, CO: Rothman & Company, 1985.

____. *Free Speech Bibliography*. New York, NY: Burt Franklin, Publisher, 1969.

____. *Free Speech for Radicals*. Reprint of 1916 edition. New York, NY: Burt Franklin, Publisher, 1970.

____. *Obscene Literature and Constitutional Law*. Reprint of 1911 edition. New York, NY: Da Capo Press, Inc., 1972.

Schwartz, Bernard. *The Great Rights of Mankind: A History of the American Bill of Rights*. New York, NY: Oxford University Press, Inc., 1977.

Seaton, Alexander A. *The Theory of Toleration under the Later Stuarts*. New York, NY: Hippocrene Books, Inc., 1972.

The SEC and the First Amendment. Washington, DC: The Media Institute, 1985.

Seldes, G. *Freedom of the Press*. Reprint of 1935 edition. New York, NY: Da Capo Press, Inc., 1971.

Shackleton, Robert. *Censure and Censorship: Impediments to Free Publication in the Age of Enlightenment*. Austin, TX: University of Texas, 1975.

Shapiro, George H., Mercurio, James P. and Kurland, Philip B. *Cablespeech: The Case for First Amendment Protection*. San Diego, CA: Harcourt Brace Jovanovich, Inc., 1984.

Shiffrin, Steven H. *The First Amendment, Democracy and Romance*. Cambridge, MA: Harvard University Press, 1990.

Shumate, T. Daniel, ed. *The First Amendment: The Legacy of George Mason*. Lanham, MD: University Publishing Associates, Inc., 1987.

Siebert, Frederick S. *Freedom of the Press in England, 1476-1776: The Rise and Decline of Government Control*. Reprint of 1965 edition. Ann Arbor, MI: Books on Demand.

_____. *The Rights and Privileges of the Press*. Reprint of 1934 edition. Westport, CT: Greenwood Publishing Group, Inc., 1970.

Silverstein, Ben. *Freedom of Information in the United States: A Bibliography*. Monticello, IL: Vance Bibliographies, 1986.

Skilling, Gordon H. *Samizdat and an Independent Society in Central and Eastern Europe*. Columbus, OH: Ohio State University Press, 1989.

Smith, Jeffrey A. *Printers and Press Freedom: The Ideology of Early American Journalism*. Reprint of 1987 edition. New York, NY: Oxford University Press, Inc., 1990.

Smith, Stephen A., ed. *Free Speech Yearbook: 1987, Vol. 26*. Carbondale, IL: Southern Illinois University Press, 1988.

Smolla, Rodney A. *Jerry Falwell v. Larry Flynt: The First Amendment on Trial*. New York, NY: St. Martin's Press, 1988.

_____. *Suing the Press*. New York, NY: Oxford University Press, Inc., 1987.

Snitow, Ann B., et al. *Powers of Desire: The Politics of Sexuality*. New York, NY: Monthly Review Press, 1983.

Soble, Alan. *Pornography: Marxism, Feminism and the Future of Sexuality.* New Haven, CT: Yale University Press, 1986.

Spitzer, Matthew L. *Seven Dirty Words and Six Other Stories: Controlling the Content of Print and Broadcast.* New Haven, CT: Yale University Press, 1987.

Stanek, Lou W. *Censorship: A Guide for Teachers, Librarians, and Others Concerned with Intellectual Freedom.* New York, NY: Dell Publishing Company, Inc.

Steigleman, Walter A. *The Newspaper and the Law.* Reprint of 1950 edition. Westport, CT: Greenwood Publishing Group, Inc., 1971.

Stephen, L. *Essays on Freethinking and Plainspeaking.* Reprint of 1905 edition. New York, NY: AMS Press, Inc.

Stevens, John D. *Shaping the First Amendment: The Development of Free Expression.* Beverly Hills, CA: Sage Publications, 1982.

Stewart, James B., ed. *The Constitution, the Law and Freedom of Expression: 1787-1987.* Carbondale, IL: Southern Illinois University Press, 1987.

Student Press Law Center. *Law of the Student Press.* Washington, DC: Student Press Law Center, Inc., 1985.

Summers, Harrison B., ed. *Radio Censorship.* History of Broadcasting: Radio to Television Series. Reprint of 1939 edition. Salem, NH: Ayer Company Publishers, Inc., 1971.

Sussman, Leonard R. *Power, the Press and the Technology of Freedom: The Coming Age of ISDN.* New York, NY: Freedom House, 1989.

Sutherland, John. *Offensive Literature: Decensorship in Britain, 1960-1982.* Savage, MD: Barnes and Noble Books-Imports, 1983.

Tanner, Henry. *Martyrdom of Lovejoy: An Account of the Life, Trials, and Perils of Rev. Elijah P. Lovejoy.* Reprint of 1881 edition. New York, NY: Augustus M. Kelley Publishers, 1971.

Tedford, Thomas L., et al., eds. *Freedom of Speech in the United States*. New York, NY: Random House, 1985.

____. *Perspectives on Freedom of Speech: Selected Essays from the Journals of the Speech Communication Association.* Carbondale, IL: Southern Illinois University Press, 1987.

Terrou, Fernand and Solal, Lucien. *Legislation for Press, Film and Radio: Comparative Study of the Main Types of Regulations Governing the Information Media*. Reprint of 1951 edition. Salem, NH: Ayer Company Publishers, Inc., 1972.

Thomson, John. *Enquiry Concerning the Liberty and Licentiousness of the Press*. Reprint of 1801 edition. New York, NY: Da Capo Press, Inc., 1970.

Tucker, D.F. *Law, Liberalism and Free Speech*. Totowa, NJ: Rowman and Allanheld, 1986.

Twentieth Century Fund, Task Force Report for a National News Council Staff. *A Free and Responsive Press*. Reprint of 1973 edition. Millwood, NY: Kraus Reprint and Periodicals.

Ungar, Sanford J. *The Papers and the Papers: An Account of the Legal and Political Battle over the Pentagon Papers*. New York, NY: Columbia University Press, 1989.

United States Government. *Report of the Commission on Obscenity and Pornography*. New York, NY: Bantam, 1970.

Van Alstyne, William. *Interpretations of the First Amendment*. Durham, NC: Duke University Press, 1984.

Van Niekerk, Barend. *The Cloistered Virtue: Freedom of Speech and the Administration of Justice in the Western World*. New York, NY: Praeger Publishers, 1987.

Vernau, Judi, ed. *Index to 'Index on Censorship.'* New York, NY: K.G. Saur, 1989.

Wagman, Robert J. *First Amendment Book*. New York, NY: Pharos Books, 1991.

Weatherby, W.J. *Salman Rushdie: Sentenced to Death*. New York, NY: Carroll and Graf Publishers, 1990.

Weinberger, Harry. *The Liberty of the Press*. New York, NY: Gordon Press Publishers.

Wells, Clare. *The UN, UNESCO and the Politics of Knowledge*. New York, NY: Macmillan Publishing Company, 1987.

West, Mark I. *Trust Your Children: Voices Against Censorship in Children's Literature*. New York, NY: Neal-Schuman Publishers, 1988.

Wickwar, William H. *The Struggle for Freedom of the Press, 1819-1832*. Reprint of 1928 edition. New York, NY: Johnson Reprint Corporation.

Woods, L.B. *A Decade of Censorship in America: The Threat to Classrooms and Libraries, 1966-1975*. Metuchen, NJ: Scarecrow Press, Inc., 1979.

Wortman, Tunis. *Treatise Concerning Political Enquiry and the Liberty of the Press*. Reprint of 1800 edition. New York, NY: Da Capo Press, Inc., 1970.

Wright, R. George. *The Future of Free Speech Law*. Westport, CT: Greenwood Publishing Group, Inc., 1990.

Zerman, Melvyn B. *Taking on the Press: Constitutional Rights in Conflict*. New York, NY: Harper Collins Children's Books, 1986.

American Booksellers Foundation for Free Expression

OFFICERS AND DIRECTORS, 1991–1992

PRESIDENT

Oren J. Teicher
American Booksellers Association
560 White Plains Road
Tarrytown, NY 10591
(800) 637-0037

VICE PRESIDENT

Chuck Robinson
Village Books
1210 11th Street
Bellingham, WA 98225
(206) 671-2626

SECRETARY-TREASURER

Bernard E. Rath
American Booksellers Association
560 White Plains Road
Tarrytown, NY 10591
(800) 637-0037

DIRECTORS*

Daniel W. Chartrand
Water Street Bookstore
125 Water Street
Exeter, NH 03833
(603) 778-9731

James L. Dana
The Bookman
715 Washington Street
Grand Haven, MI 49417
(616) 846-3520

Deborah D. Garman
Route 1, Box 219–B
Banks, OR 97106
(503) 324-8180

Rhett Jackson
The Happy Bookseller
4525 Forest Drive
Columbia, SC 29206
(803) 787-3136

Lisa Knudsen
Mountains and Plains
  Booksellers Association
805 La Porte Avenue
Fort Collins, CO 80521
(303) 484-5856

Max Lillienstein
Cooperman Levitt &
  Winikoff, P.C.
800 Third Avenue
New York, NY 10022
(212) 688-7000

Melissa J. Mytinger
Northern California
  Booksellers Association
1339 61st Street
Emeryville, CA 94608
(510) 601-6922

Larry Robin
Robin's Bookstore
108 South 13th Street
Philadelphia, PA 19107
(215) 735-9598

Susan E. Walker
Upper Midwest
  Booksellers Association
4018 West 65th Street
Edina, MN 55435
(612) 926-4102

---

* Board Members serve as individuals, not necessarily as representatives of the organizations with which they are affiliated.

Know Your Opposition

A LIST OF PROMINENT GROUPS OPPOSED TO FREE EXPRESSION

T his list provides the names and addresses of some of the largest and most active groups involved in the restriction of freedom of expression. These organizations are well-run, and careful not to define themselves as "pro-censorship." Often, they defend their actions by claiming to act in the best interests of children, the family, and American values.

In order to better understand and combat the way these organizations work, try to obtain copies of as much of their paperwork as possible—letters to you, letters from the leadership to the followers, press releases, newsletters, proposed legislation, and flyers. The more information you have, the better you can plan your response.

This list is by no means all-inclusive. A number of socially responsible organizations may, at times, adopt restrictive stances on issues of free expression in an attempt to remove reading material, films, videotapes, recordings, etc., that they feel foster some sort of antisocial behavior. Whether acting on a local level through individual chapters of larger organizations or mobilizing nationally on a single issue, these groups should also be reminded of the need to preserve and protect our First Amendment rights.

American Family Association
Box 2440
Tupelo, MS 38803
(601) 844-5036

The Berean League
2875 Snelling Avenue North
St. Paul, MN 55113-7199
(612) 633-0654

Caleb Campaign
P.O. Box 173
Algonquin, IL 60102
(618) 942-7520

Christian Coalition
P.O. Box 1990
Chesapeake, VA 23320
(804) 424-2630

Concerned Women
for America
370 L'Enfant Promenade SW
Suite 800
Washington, DC 20024
(202) 488-7000

Eagle Forum
P.O. Box 618
Alton, IL 62002
(618) 462-5415

Educational Research
Analysts
P.O. Box 7518
Longview, TX 75607
(214) 453-3993

Focus on the Family
P.O. Box 500
Pomona, CA 91799

Institute for Creation
Research
P.O. Box 2667
El Cajon, CA 92021

National Association of
Christian Educators/
Citizens for Excellence
in Education
P.O. Box 3200
Costa Mesa, CA 92628
(719) 546-5931

National Coalition Against
Pornography
800 Compton Road
Suite 9248
Cincinnati, OH 45231

The Rutherford Institute
P.O. Box 7482
Charlottesville, VA 22906

Significant Court Cases Involving First Amendment Rights

T he following are selected noteworthy First Amendment cases. They are arranged by year of decision and involve cases handed down at a variety of court levels, for example, U.S. Supreme Court, Courts of Appeal, District Courts, as well as state supreme and appellate courts.

The legal citation is included to help those who wish to locate the original court decision. For example, the citation *Schenck* v. *United States*, 249 U.S. 47 (1919), provides the following information: the name of the case, with the party appealing to the Court first, and the other listed second (*Schenck* v. *United States*); the volume number (249); the name of the publication (U.S. is *United States Reports*); the page number (47); and the year the case was decided (1919).

Abbreviations:

U.S. = *United States Reports*
S.Ct. = *Supreme Court Reporter*
L.Ed. = *United States Supreme Court Reports Lawyers' Edition*
L.Ed.2d = *United States Supreme Court Reports Lawyers' Edition, Second Series*
P. = *Pacific Reporter*
N.Y.S. = *New York Supplement*

N.W. = *North Western Reporter*
F.2d = *Federal Reporter, Second Series*
F.Supp. = *Federal Supplement*

Schenck v. United States, 249 U.S. 47 (1919)

This is the famous case in which Oliver Wendell Holmes declared, for the first time in a Supreme Court decision, that the First Amendment does not protect all speech. To illustrate his point he gave the famous example of not being allowed to cry "fire" in a crowded theater. Having so stated, he went on to formulate the now-famous "clear and present danger test" for determining which speech would be protected and which would not. "The question," he declared, "in every case is whether the words are used in certain circumstances ... as to create a clear and present danger that they will bring about the substantive evils that Congress has the right to prevent."

Gitlow v. New York, 268 U.S. 652 (1925)

Ironically, in a decision *restricting* speech by upholding a state law making it a crime to advocate the overthrow of government, the Supreme Court ruled for the first time that the First Amendment applied to all levels of government, rather than just the Federal Government. Stating: "For present purposes we may and do assume that freedom of speech and of the press—which are protected by the First Amendment from abridgement by Congress—are among the fundamental personal rights and 'liberties' protected by the due process clause of the Fourteenth Amendment from impairment by the states." This ruling was of great importance in upholding of First Amendment rights in that state and local laws restricting speech were now subject to the Bill of Rights and the Constitution.

Near v. Minnesota, 283 U.S. 697 (1931)

This was the first time that the Supreme Court declared "prior restraint" to be a violation of the First Amendment. A prior restraint is an injunction or other pre-publication restraint on the dissemination of speech. The *Near* decision was relied upon in 1971 when the Supreme Court declared the attempt by the U.S. Government to enjoin the *New York Times* from publishing classified documents about the Vietnam War to be unconstitutional. (See *New York Times* v. *United States*.)

Joseph Burstyn, Inc. v. Wilson, 343 U.S. 495, 72 S. Ct. (1952)

The New York Board of Regents had denied a license to exhibit a motion picture, Roberto Rossellini's "The Miracle," on the basis of its opinion that the film was "sacrilegious." The Supreme Court overruled, stating that film is "a significant medium for the communication of ideas." The Court further ruled that "Motion pictures are within the ambit of the constitutional guarantees of freedom of speech and of the press." In doing so, film was for the first time considered to be protected speech.

Butler v. Michigan, 352 U.S. 380 (1957)

The Supreme Court overruled an obscenity conviction based upon a law banning sexually explicit materials which would be harmful to children. This is the opinion in which the Court in a famous footnote characterized the law as "burning the barn in order to roast the pig."

Roth v. United States, 354 U.S. 476, 77 S. Ct. (1957)

Roth reversed a ruling which had found a publication obscene "because it tended to cause immoral thoughts in minds open to such influences." The Court, rejecting the previous test of obscenity set out in *Regina (Queen of England)* v. *Hicklin,* L.R. 3 Q.B. 360 (1863), stated what it considered had become the standard judicial test of obscenity: "whether to the average person, applying contemporary community standards, the dominant theme of the material taken as a whole appeals to prurient interests." The Court acknowledged First Amendment protection of works embodying "ideas having even the slightest redeeming social importance—unorthodox ideas, controversial ideas, even ideas hateful to the prevailing climate of opinion—[which] have the full protection of the [First Amendment] guaranties, unless excludable because they encroach upon the limited area of more important interests." However, the Court added that, "implicit in the history of the First Amendment is the rejection of obscenity as utterly without redeeming social importance, ... obscenity is not within the area of constitutionally protected speech or press." The *Roth* test of "utterly without redeeming social value" was later rejected in *Miller* v. *California* (1973). *Miller* also refined the *Roth* concept of "community standards."

Kingsley Int'l Pictures Corp. v. Regents of the Univ. of N.Y., 360 U.S. 684 (1959)

In *Kingsley* the decision of a New York court was reversed which had denied a license to show the film "Lady Chatterley's Lover." The Court stated (at 688-689): "what New York has done ... is to prevent the exhibition of a motion picture because that picture advocates an idea—that adultery under certain circumstances may be proper behavior.... [The First Amendment's] guarantee is not confined to the expression of ideas that are conventional or shared by a majority. It protects advocacy of the opinion that adultery may sometimes be proper, no less than advocacy of socialism or the single tax." The court proclaimed that the film, in "dealing with sex in a manner that advocates ideas, ... may not be branded as obscenity" and denied constitutional protection.

New York Times v. Sullivan, 376 U.S. 254 (1964)

From the perspective of publishers, distributors and retailers of books, magazines and newspapers and other expressive materials, this may very well constitute the most important First Amendment decision handed down by the Court. Here the Court held that material published with regard to "public officials" could not constitutionally be deemed libelous unless it was published or disseminated with "actual malice." The Court then went on to define "actual malice" as material that the public official can prove was "known to be false" by the disseminator of the statement or "that it was made with reckless disregard for the truth."

Jacobellis v. Ohio, 378 U.S. 184 (1964)

Jacobellis, manager of a Cleveland movie theater, had been convicted for possessing and exhibiting an obscene film in violation of Ohio law. The conviction was reversed in this ruling. The question before the Supreme Court was whether the state courts had correctly found the film "Les Amants" ("The Lovers") to be obscene and therefore unprotected by the First Amendment. In *Jacobellis* the court reaffirmed its findings in *Roth* v. *United States* (1957) and *Alberts* v. *California* (1957) that "Application of an obscenity law to suppress a motion picture thus require ascertainment of the 'dim and uncertain line' that often separates obscenity from constitutionally protected expression."

A Book Named "John Cleland's Memoirs of a Woman of Pleasure (Fanny Hill)" v. Attorney General of Massachusetts, 383 U.S. 413 (1966)

This case overruled a state court decision upholding the banning of the book "Fanny Hill" as "prurient and offensive" even though it might have "some minimal literary value." In a further refinement of *Roth*, the Supreme Court ruled that publications could be banned only when all three of the following applied: "1) the dominant theme of the material taken as a whole appeals to a prurient interest; 2) the material is patently offensive to community standards; 3) the material is 'utterly without redeeming social importance.'" This three part test would be further refined in *Miller* v. *California*.

Tinker v. Des Moines School District, 393 U.S. 503 (1969)

This case was important for holding that minors, even in the environment of a public school, possess First Amendment rights to express political and social views. The Court went on to hold that by wearing black arm bands during the Vietnam

War the students were simply using symbolic speech to protest that war and that such speech was protected.

New York Times v. United States, 403 U.S. 713 (1971)

This is probably the most famous First Amendment case in the history of the Supreme Court. The U.S. Government attempted to enjoin the *New York Times* and the *Washington Post* from publishing certain classified documents about the Vietnam War, which were referred to as the "Pentagon Papers." The Court did indicate that under certain circumstances, where publication might seriously interfere with foreign policy or affect the ability of our government to conduct a war, publication might be enjoined. However, the Court found any such claims in this case to be unpersuasive.

Miller v. California, 413 U.S. 15 (1973)

Fourteen years after the decision in *Roth* v. *United States*, in which the Supreme Court first defined "obscenity" and held that it was not protected by the First Amendment, the Court adopted a somewhat different definition containing a three-pronged test. Material would not be deemed "obscene" unless "taken as a whole" the "average person," when applying contemporary community standards, would find:

(a) the material appeals primarily to the "prurient" interests;

(b) it depicts or describes, in a particularly offensive way, physical conduct proscribed by state or Federal law; and

(c) the work is lacking in "serious literary, artistic and scientific value."

Gertz v. Robert Welch, Inc., 418 U.S. 323 (1974)

This case extended the rule in *New York Times* v. *Sullivan* to "public figures." It held that any public figure must prove "actual malice" before a libel action could prevail. The plaintiff was a prominent lawyer who contended that he was libeled by a leaflet. (See *New York Times* v. *Sullivan*.)

Island Trees School District v. Pico, 457 U.S. 853 (1982)

The Supreme Court in 1975 held, for the first time, that a school board could not remove books from a public school library "simply because they disliked the ideas contained in those books and seek by their removal to prescribe what shall be orthodox in politics, nationalism, religion or other matters of opinion." The Court very carefully asserted the right of public schools to inculcate in its students "traditional" values, thereby casting a great deal of uncertainty upon how far public schools could go in consciously attempting to shape a student's political, social, nationalistic or other views.

New York v. Ferber, 458 U.S. 747 (1982)

This was the first case in which the Supreme Court held that the publication, production and/or dissemination of sexually explicit but non-obscene materials could be criminalized. The Court held that the standard of obscenity set forth in *Miller* v. *California* need not be applied where child pornography is involved. Instead, the test under *Ferber* requires a finding that the objectionable material involves the use of a minor as a model or performer in a photograph or motion picture involving "actual or simulated sexual intercourse, deviate sexual intercourse, bestiality, masturbation, sado-masochistic abuse, or lewd exhibition of the genitals." In a plurality opinion, Justice White declared, nevertheless, that any such material that had serious literary, scientific or educational value was protected under the First Amendment. The case was important not so much for the facts therein involved, but because it created an additional exception to the absolute language of the First Amendment. It is also important because it is the first case involving sexually explicit material where the Court was concerned primarily with the effect on models or performers used in the production of the material and not on the offensive effect the material might have in the community at large.

ABA v. Hudnut, ___ U.S. ___ (1986), *aff'g without opinion* 771 F.2d 323 (7th Cir.) 1985

This case tested the constitutionality of an Indiana ordinance which banned sexually explicit materials which were "demeaning to women." The Court held the ordinance unconstitutional on the ground that it was so broad in its application that it would include within its scope many non-obscene books. To that extent the ordinance attempted to ban ideas that the legislature found offensive, something the First Amendment cannot abide.

Smith v. Mobile County, 827 F.2d 684 (1987)

The Eleventh Circuit Court of Appeals held that 44 different elementary through high school textbooks need not be removed from the curriculum simply because certain parents and their children were offended by matter in those books, believed to be teaching the religion of "secular humanism." Conceding that some of the ideas in the books might be ideas shared by one or more religious groups, the Court found it was not necessary therefore to ban those books as being in violation of the "free expression" and "establishment" clauses of the First Amendment. The Court further found that the textbooks neither advanced a non-theistic religion nor inhibited theistic religions.

Mozert v. Hawkins, 827 F.2d 1058 (1987)

The Sixth Circuit Court of Appeals held in *Mozert* that certain standard reading textbooks did not have to be withdrawn from the curriculum simply because some of the secular views expressed in those books were offensive to the religious beliefs of certain parents and their children. The parents had sought the right to teach reading at home from texts the parents would select.

Hazelwood v. Kuhlmeier, 484 U.S. 260 (1988)

A school principal had removed two pages containing an article on teenage pregnancy and an article on the impact of divorce on students from a school newspaper produced by the high school journalism class. The Supreme Court held that since the speech in question was produced on school grounds, with school funds and as part of the regular journalism curriculum, it was subject to control by the faculty. It rejected a claim that by authorizing the creation of the newspaper, the school had created a public forum from which all student speech would be protected by the First Amendment. This case was a great disappointment to proponents of the students' right to free expression, who believed that *Tinker* v. *Des Moines* would have protected the right of these students to publish these articles in the school newspaper.

ABA v. Virginia, ___ U.S. ___ (1988)

This was the first time the Supreme Court was asked to deny the constitutionality of a minors' access statute. Virginia had enacted a law criminalizing the sale of materials that were "harmful to minors." Harmful to minors was defined in such a way that it was susceptible to an interpretation that would clearly have proscribed protected materials. Rather than deal directly with the issue, the Supreme Court certified two questions to the Supreme Court of Virginia for the purpose of obtaining an interpretation by the Highest Court of Virginia as to the precise meaning of the statute. The Virginia court so narrowly construed the statute that in effect it would include within its scope "virtually the same materials that would be proscribed under the state's obscenity laws." Thus narrowed, the Fourth Circuit Court of Appeals, when the case was remanded to it by the Supreme Court of the United States, held that the Virginia minors' access statute was constitutional.

Ft. Wayne Books, Inc. v. Indiana, ___ U.S. ___ (1989)

In this case, the Supreme Court held that an Indiana RICO statute which was made applicable to the sale of obscene materials could be used so as to permit the authorities to seize all the assets of the accused without a judicial hearing. The Supreme Court reversed on the ground that such a seizure constituted a prior restraint barred by the First Amendment.

Texas v. Johnson, ___ U.S. ___ (1989)

This is the first of the now famous "flag burning" cases holding that no matter how offensive speech is, including the symbolic speech involved in burning an American flag, it is protected by the First Amendment.

FTC v. Sable Communications, Inc., ___ U.S. ___ (1990)

Here the Supreme Court held that a law banning "indecent" telephone communications was so broad that it would clearly apply to protected, as well as unprotected, speech. Despite pleas that the law was intended to protect minors, the Court held that it would be an unconstitutional abridgement of speech.

Rust v. Sullivan, ___ U.S. ___ (1991)

In this highly significant decision, the Supreme Court held that federal regulations banning the giving of advice regarding abortion at any clinic or facility subsidized by federal funds was a constitutional application of the government's power to grant subsidies. Many critics of the ruling have pointed out that, if carried to its logical extreme, the Federal Government could control the conduct of books, magazines and other expressive materials in public libraries, public schools and other institutions and facilities that are wholly, or partially, subsidized by the government.

ABA v. Webb, ___ Fed.2d ___ (11th Cir. 1991)

ABA and other plaintiffs challenged the constitutionality of minors' access statutes that were similar in form to statutes in a number of other states. The District Court held the statutes unconstitutional. But after various appeals to the 11th Circuit Court of Appeals, that court finally held, following the decision in *ABA* v. *Virginia*, that the Georgia statute was constitutional. It narrowly construed the statute, however, so that it had little application to works other than those that would be deemed obscene under *Miller* v. *California*.

This chapter was prepared by ABA counsel Max Lillienstein, of Cooperman, Levitt & Winikoff, P.C., New York, NY.

Handling Complaints

SAMPLE STORE PROCEDURE FOR HANDLING CONTENT-BASED COMPLAINTS

T he following procedure, contributed by James Dana and the Great Lakes Booksellers Association, has several objectives: to provide a consistent and orderly way to deal with content-based complaints; to provide staff with the security and confidence to meet such complaints in an appropriate way; to provide management with enough time and information to respond effectively and appropriately; and to ascertain the seriousness of the complaint by requiring that the complainant show that he or she has also given the matter serious consideration. It is assumed that initially, at least, the complaint is made in person. For complaints by phone or mail, the procedure should be adjusted accordingly.

Procedure

In the event of a complaint about the appropriateness of stocking a particular item or of its location or merchandising, take the following steps, in order:

1. Remain courteous, listen to the customer's objection.

2. Examine the facts. Perhaps a book was shelved in the wrong section, contrary to policy. In such a case, simply rectify the situation. However, if the book was shelved correctly, according to normal practice and policies, do not do, or offer to do, anything with it, including temporary removal from the shelves or shifting to another location.

3. If the book was properly shelved, explain store policy to the customer. Do not, however, engage in an argument or allow yourself to be drawn into trying to justify the presence of specific titles in the store except in light of the store policy. Also avoid being drawn into giving your personal judgment of the "appropriateness" of inclusion or merchandising of specific titles in the inventory. Avoid being drawn into characterizing specific titles with such highly-charged and subjective terms as "pornographic," "obscene," or "blasphemous." Notify the manager of the complaint and how you handled it.

4. If the customer is not satisfied with the explanation of store policy and wants further action or discussion, refer the matter to the manager with a statement such as: "I'm sorry, but I am not authorized to take any action on such matters. You'll have to discuss that with the manager."

5. Contact the manager. If the manager is not available, ask the customer to fill out the complaint form.

6. The manager should attempt to elicit the information called for in the complaint form, or simply ask the customer to fill it out.

7. After receiving a detailed complaint, the manager should:

- notify the customer that no change will be made, if that is clearly the right course, or
- inform the customer that the complaint will be considered and the customer informed of the decision.

8. Consult with other management—ABA, MBA, ABFFE, Media Coalition, your lawyer, etc.—as appropriate.

9. Decide on the proper disposition of the complaint.

10. Make any changes. Notify the complainant of the disposition.

SAMPLE COMPLAINT FORM

It has been standard practice in libraries for some time to use a complaint form in handling complaints. The reasons for this are several: it requires that the complainants show that they really understand what it is they are complaining about; it requires that the complainants say clearly what they think is wrong and what remedy they would like to see; these requirements themselves often defuse a situation; and it slows the process down, thereby ensuring that the library gives the matter due consideration before deciding on and taking any course of action. For these same reasons, bookstores might find it a useful practice to adopt. Feel free to use the following form as is, or adapt it to your store's requirements.

Complaint initiated by _____

Address _____

_____

Telephone Number _____

Complainant represents: Himself/Herself _____

Name of Organization _____

_____

Date _____

Book Title_____

Author_____

Publisher_____

1. Why do you object to this book?_____

_____

2. To what do you specifically object (cite pages)? _____

3. What do you think might be the result of reading this book?_____

_____

4. For what age group would you recommend this book?

_____

5. Is there anything good about this book?_____

_____

6. Did you read the entire book?   _____

If not, what parts?   _____

7. What do you believe is the theme or purpose of this book?

_____

_____

8. Are you aware of the judgment of this book by critics or others in the field?   _____

9. What reviews of the book have you seen?   _____

_____

10. What would you like [Store Name] to do about this book?_____

_____

Date_____

Signature_____

Complaint received by _____

Action Taken _____

_____

_____

Ten Commandments for the Fight Against Censorship*

BY DAVE MARSH

1. *Emphasize the Positive.* The censors do NOT have the right to define the agenda and pick the battleground. Aggressively expose the history of what censorship has done to ruin democracy in countries all over the world. Insist that the greatest peril to our children's education and morals is ignorance and the denial of reality. Remind everyone that unpleasant social realities can't be solved until we all have the right to say openly what's on our minds. Never forget that free speech advocates are parents, good citizens, and (often) good Christians too.

2. *You Don't Have to Spend Your Life Living Like a Refugee.* The majority of Americans *are* moral; they're also in favor of free speech. A July 1990 *Newsweek* poll showed that 75 percent of Americans felt that the right of adults to "determine what they may see and hear" was "more important" than society having "laws to prohibit material that may be offensive to some segments of the community." So, don't shut up—you don't just have the *privilege* of free speech, you have the *right* to speak, and when that right is threatened, speaking out becomes an *obligation*.

3. *On the Other Hand, Remember This:* The First Amendment exists to protect speech and activities that are *un*popular. If it

---

*Reprinted with permission from Dave Marsh, *50 Ways to Fight Censorship*, published by Thunder's Mouth Press (New York, 1991).

only served to protect that which everybody (or "the majority") agreed with, it wouldn't need to be there at all. Limiting free speech is what's *un*American—without it all our other rights and liberties quickly disintegrate. That's why it's the *First* Amendment.

That also means that it's imperative to support independent sources of culture in all the arts, especially given the growing concentration of the publishing, music, and film industries in the hands of a small number of corporate interests. The artists, retailers, and others fighting hardest for free expression tend to be those outside the mainstream of the system. For some art forms—avant garde poetry, the blues, and documentaries, for instance—the independent publishers, record labels, and film distributors provide virtually the only means of existence. So where you have a choice, shop and browse on that basis.

4. *Don't Believe the Hype.* Don't let censors claim they aren't censoring; if it restricts freedom of expression, it's against the First Amendment. One of the most important lessons that censors have learned over the years is never to use the word "censorship." But, as Ali Mazrui wrote in *The Black Scholar*, "Censorship in the U.S. is basically privatized...freelance censors abound."

Censorship isn't about intentions; it's about consequences. Whether they're presented as "consumer information" or "child protection" or "public safety" (as in the refusal of civic facilities to allow certain kinds of performances to take place), regulations and activities that deny the right to speak ARE forms of censorship, no matter what name their sponsors give them.

5. *Freedom Isn't Free.* The majority of censorship is *economic*, which forces artists to work day jobs to stay alive, and prevents them from creating freely, let alone acquiring the equipment to work with and the space to work in.

Turn some of the ideas in this book into fundraisers. Use the money you receive to publish and distribute free speech information, to take out anti-censorship ads, to develop and produce free speech public service announcements, and for the legal expenses of those who are censored.

6. Keep Your Sense of Humor. This will immediately distinguish you from the censors, who don't have any. Censorship fanatics *never* tell jokes about the issue; they never let the air out of their own bags of wind. Don't be afraid to help them out—or to deflate your own gasbag once in a while.

7. Remember the Commandment the Censors Forgot: "Thou shalt not bear false witness against thy neighbors." That doesn't just mean don't lie; it means get the facts straight. So go after those half-truths and expose the lies the censors promote. Make yourself so well-informed that you'll *know* when censors are fabricating facts or distorting "scientific studies," or when they're refusing to acknowledge common sense. If you doubt what they're saying, make 'em *prove* what they're saying is so, and don't let them bluster and bully with anecdotes that never involve names, dates, or places.

8. Don't Mourn. Organize seminars and study groups to look at censorship in context; accept no easy answers. Find out where attacks on free speech are coming from—even if it means going back 100 or even 500 years. It's important to see both censored and uncensored art. Teach yourself the history of free music, free art, free cinema, etc., so that the lies of the censors won't trick you.

9. Take Advantage of Resources—telephones, fax machines, photocopiers—wherever you can find them. It doesn't take an army to make a big difference. Jack Thompson, the Florida censor who launched a campaign that helped get 2 Live Crew indicted, did it all out of his house with a phone and a fax setup. You can fight back effectively using the same kinds of tools.

10. Contact Other Groups in Your Area that should have an interest in free speech—not just arts councils, but unions, civil rights organizations, churches, journalists, broadcasters, feminists. Make sure they understand the issue. Ask for their support — and support their causes whenever you can.

Sense and Censorship: The Vanity of Bonfires*

BY MARCIA PALLY

RESOURCE MATERIALS ON SEXUALLY EXPLICIT MATERIAL, VIOLENT MATERIAL AND CENSORSHIP: RESEARCH AND PUBLIC POLICY IMPLICATIONS

PREFACE

T he First Amendment was designed 'to invite dispute,' to induce 'a condition of unrest,' to 'create dissatisfaction with conditions as they are,' and even to stir 'people to anger.'

The First Amendment was not fashioned as a vehicle for dispensing tranquilizers to the people. Its prime function was to keep debate open to 'offensive' as well as to 'staid' people.... The materials before us may be garbage. But so is much of what is said in political campaigns, in the daily press, on TV or over the radio. By reason of the First Amendment ... speakers and publishers have not been threatened or subdued because their thoughts and ideas may be 'offensive' to some.

—Justice William O. Douglas, *Miller* v. *California*, June 6, 1973, 413 U.S. 15, p. 1453)

Supreme Court Justice William Douglas takes it as an obvious good that "speakers and publishers have not been threatened or subdued." The right to read, view and hear what one chooses has long been considered a founda-

---

*Sponsored by Americans for Constitutional Freedom and the Freedom to Read Foundation. A companion essay is available from Americans for Constitutional Freedom, 900 Third Avenue, Suite 1600, New York, NY 10022.

tion of democracy; censorship, an incursion into liberty. This right to free expression was meant most particularly, as Justice Douglas stated, to protect unpopular material, those books or films that some people believe are dangerous, blasphemous or merely offensive. The First Amendment was the linchpin behind the civil rights challenge to racial discrimination, which many Americans initially considered lunatic and anarchic. It is why Christian fundamentalists may promote their ideas about religion and a Bible-based government. It allows white supremacists to publicize their views and women to challenge sexism and gender roles—though most Americans are not Christian fundamentalists, white supremacists or feminists.

In a democracy, Adlai Stevenson II wrote, "The sound of tireless voices is the price we pay for the right to hear the music of our own opinions." Abraham Lincoln said more simply, "Those who deny freedom to others do not deserve it for themselves."

Over the last decade, it has become increasingly popular to believe that banning or restricting books, music, pictures and motion pictures is the solution to the social problems of the day. The most prevalent version of this idea promises that restricting sexually explicit material and rock and roll will rid society of drug abuse, teen pregnancy and sexual violence. Before the nation hobbles its free speech rights, it seems pertinent to ask if this proposition is true.

Below is an investigation of the psychological and sociological research on sexually explicit material, rock and social harms. The data suggest that banning or restricting sexual material and rock will not reduce violence or sexual and drug abuses, which have their sources in entrenched, complex social structures.

Drs. Edward Donnerstein, Daniel Linz and Steven Penrod, leading researchers in the field, wrote, "Should harsher penalties be leveled against persons who traffic in pornography, particularly violent pornography? We do not believe so.... The legal course of action is more restrictive of personal freedoms than an educational approach. And, as we have noted, the existing research probably does not justify this approach."

Their words recall those of Supreme Court Justice Louis Brandeis: "The threat to our liberty lies not with the evil-minded ruler—for men born to freedom are quick to resist tyranny—rather it lies with men of zeal—well-meaning, but lacking understanding."

1. COMMISSIONS

1A. The Report of the President's Commission on Obscenity and Pornography, 1970

Between 1968 and 1970, the President's Commission on Obscenity and Pornography studied the relationship between sexually explicit material and antisocial behavior. Over a two-year period with a budget of $2,000,000 (in 1970 dollars, in contrast to the $400,000–$500,000 in 1985 dollars allotted to the Meese Commission), it ran national surveys on pornography consumption and crime rates, and conducted controlled laboratory studies. The 1970 commission concluded:

"Empirical research designed to clarify the question has found no reliable evidence to date that exposure to sexual materials plays a significant role in the causation of delinquent or criminal sexual behavior among youth or adults." (1970 Commission Report, p. 139)

"Studies of juvenile delinquents indicate that their experience with erotica is generally similar to that of nondelinquents.... There is no basis in the available data however for supposing that there is any independent relationship between exposure to erotica and delinquency." (1970 Commission Report, p. 242)

"If a case is to be made against pornography in 1970, it will have to be made on grounds other than demonstrated effects of a damaging personal or social nature." (1970 Commission Report, p. 139)

- Two of the commissioners wrote:

"We would have welcomed evidence relating exposure to erotica to delinquency, crime and antisocial behavior, for if any such evidence existed we might have a simple solution to some of our most urgent problems. However, the research fails to establish a meaningful causal relationship or even significant correlation between exposure to erotica and immediate or delayed antisocial behavior among adults. To assert the contrary ... is not only to deny the facts, but also to delude the public by offering a spurious and simplistic answer to highly complex problems." (Dr. Morris Lipton and Dr. Edward Greenwood, *Psychiatric News*, March 15, 1972)

- In the years since 1970, two ideas have become popular: that pornography has become more violent and that it is responsible for antisocial behavior, most notably rape, wife battery, incest and sexual perversions. In 1985, Attorney General Edwin Meese formed another commission, now commonly called the Meese Commission, to study the social and psychological effects of sexually explicit material.

1B. The publicity surrounding Attorney General Edwin Meese's Commission on Pornography (1986) led to the belief that sexually explicit material causes sexual assault and perversions, and should be restricted from circulation to the public.

In fact: The Meese Commission's investigation of the social science data does not support this conclusion.

- Dr. Park Dietz, a member of the Meese Commission and medical director of the Institute of Law, Psychiatry and Public Policy at the University of Virginia, said:

"I believe that *Playboy* centerfolds are among the healthiest sexual images in America, and so are many of Mr. Guccione's centerfolds."

● Henry Hudson, chairman of the Meese Commission, said:

"A lot of critics think that our report focuses on publications like *Playboy* and *Penthouse* and that is totally untrue."

● Dr. Frederick Schauer, a member of the Meese Commission, author of the draft document that served as a basis for the Meese Commission report, and professor of law at the University of Michigan, wrote:

"I do not make the claim, nor does the report, that the category of sexually explicit material bears a causal relationship to acts of sexual violence. I do not make the claim, nor does the report, that the degree of explicitness is relevant in explaining the causal relationship between depictions of sexual violence and acts of sexual violence.... As the evidence so clearly indicates, and as the report so clearly, and in italics, states, the causal relationship is independent of the degree of sexual explicitness....

"The report itself never even hints at expanding the area of permissible regulation beyond that permitted by *Miller* [current law regarding obscene materials] and its associated cases.... Although I can appreciate symbolic reasons for regulating the tiny sliver of the sexually violent that is obscene ... I can appreciate as well that the marginal symbolic advantages ... would not outweigh the costs. Thus I do not find the possibility of total deregulation troublesome, and I never have." (*American Bar Foundation Research Journal*, 1987, vol. 737, pp. 767–769)

1C. The Meese Commission requested that an independent review of the social science data be prepared by Dr. Edna Einsiedel (University of Calgary).

In fact: Dr. Einsiedel's review found no link between sexually explicit material and sex crimes, and did not support the conclusions or the policy recommendations that the Meese Commission later made.

"Unfortunately," wrote Dr. Larry Baron (Yale, University of New Hampshire), "the commission paid little attention to the excellent review of the empirical literature that was prepared by the staff social scientist, Edna Einsiedel.... It would be instructive for those unfamiliar with the research on pornography to read Einsiedel's comprehensive literature review and then read [Commissioner Frederick] Schauer's deceptive executive summary." (*Society*, 1987, vol. 24, no. 5, p. 8)

1D. After Dr. Einsiedel submitted her report, the Meese Commission asked Surgeon General C. E. Koop to gather more social science data. Koop conducted a conference of researchers and practitioners in medicine, psychology and sociology to investigate the effects of pornography.

In fact: The Report of the Surgeon General's Workshop on Pornography and Public Health, 1986, found no evidence that exposure to sexual material leads to sex crimes.

• "Pornography has been consistently linked to changes in some perceptions, attitudes and behaviors. These links, however, are circumscribed, few in number and generally laboratory-based.... For instance, while it is a common belief that attitude changes lead to behavioral changes, research has consistently shown otherwise. Behaviors are as likely to influence attitudes as attitudes are to influence behavior." (Surgeon General's Report, p. 35)

• The Surgeon General's conference came to five conclusions about sexually explicit material that the research supports "with confidence."

(1) Children and adolescents who participate in the production of pornography experience adverse effects. (p. 13) In remedy, the conference called for "innovative programs to address the particular needs of a broad group of disenfranchised youth.... The reality of the situation is that someone has to go onto the street and establish programs that appeal to the youth there." (p. 55)

(2) "Prolonged use of pornography increases belief that less common sexual practices are more common." (p. 17)

The report concluded, "The estimates [of frequency of sexual practices] of the intermediate- and massive-exposure groups [to pornography] were actually more accurate than the no exposure group, which underestimated the prevalence of these behaviors." (p. 17)

(3) Pornography that portrays sexual aggression as pleasurable for the victim increases the acceptance of the use of coercion in sexual relations within the lab setting. (p. 19)

The report concluded, "It is important to remain aware, however, that the observed attitude changes are generally restricted to exposure using depictions of sexually violent incidents in which the victim becomes aroused as a result of the attack. *Attitude changes from exposure to violence or sexually explicit behavior alone are not consistently observed.*" (emphasis added, p. 22)

(4) "Acceptance of coercive sexuality appears to be related to sexual aggression." (p. 23)

"The association between attitudes and behavior in this area is one of the most difficult to comment upon conclusively.... It cannot be said presently that these attitudes *are* causally related to this [sexually aggressive] behavior. Moreover, it is not clear that exposure to pornography is the most significant factor in the development of these attitudes." (p. 23)

"An unresolved issue is whether these attitudes led to different [abusive] behavior patterns or whether the attitudes were adopted after the subject's behavior patterns were already established." (p. 25)

One study investigated attitudes about women and real-life aggression.

(Suzanne Ageton, *Sexual Assault Among Adolescents*, 1983, Lexington, Massachusetts, Lexington Books, p. 119) It found that involvement in a delinquent peer group appeared consistently as the most powerful factor, accounting for 76 percent of sexual aggression. Three other factors, including attitudes about women and violence, accounted for 19 percent altogether. (See also Surgeon General's Report, p. 27)

(5) "In laboratory studies ... exposure to violent pornography increases punitive behavior toward women. An increase in aggressive behavior toward women has been proposed often as one likely effect of exposure to pornography, but there does not seem to be sufficient scientific support for a generalized statement regarding the presence of this effect." (emphasis added, pp. 28–29)

"Reports of this causal relationship being a noticeable one in the real world have not emerged consistently. In sum, these experiments should heighten concern that aggressive behavior toward women may be increased by viewing aggressive and sexually aggressive films, but presently this effect has only been seen in controlled and potentially artificial laboratory settings." (p. 34)

1E. The publicity surrounding the Meese Commission suggested that independent social science researchers agreed on the causal link between sexually explicit material and harms.

In fact: Responses to the Meese Commission by researchers in the social sciences show they have little confidence in the commission's use of the scientific data.

● When the Meese Commission recommended the restriction of sexually explicit material, two commissioners, Dr. Judith Becker and Ellen Levine, so disagreed with the recommendations that they issued a dissenting report.

Lambasting the commission for a "paucity of certain types of testimony, including dissenting expert opinion" they concluded, "No self-respecting investigator would accept conclusions based on such a study." (Becker and Levine, Dissenting Report, pp. 4, 7)

Dr. Becker, who is also director of the Sexual Behavior Clinic at New York State Psychiatric Institute, told *The New York Times*, "I've been working with sex offenders for ten years and have reviewed the scientific literature and I don't think a causal link exists between pornography and sex crimes." (*The New York Times*, May 17, 1986)

● Dr. Edward Donnerstein (University of Wisconsin, University of California), one of the leading researchers in the area of human sexuality and one of the authorities most frequently cited by the Meese Commission, called the commission's conclusions "bizarre." (*The New York Times*, May 17, 1986)

In 1986 and 1987, Donnerstein and Drs. Daniel Linz (University of California) and Steven Penrod (University of Wisconsin) wrote several articles and a book, *The Question of Pornography: Research Findings and Policy Implications* (1987, New York, The Free Press, a division of Macmillan Inc.), examining the commission's conclusions. Summarizing their views in a December 1986 *Psychology Today* article, Donnerstein and Linz wrote:

"We feel it necessary to point out that the report fell short of our expectations in several important respects. First there are factual problems.... Several of the contentions made in its pages cannot be supported by empirical evidence.... It must be concluded that violent images, rather than sexual ones, are most responsible for people's attitudes about women and rape." (pp. 56, 59)

In their book and in subsequent reports, Donnerstein and Linz have clarified their data on sexually violent material, saying it is accurate "as long as we are referring to laboratory studies of aggression.... Whether this aggression ... is representative of real-world aggression, such as rape, is entirely a different matter." (1990 report to the government of New Zealand, p. 38)

● The same month as the Meese Commission completed its hearings, Dr. David Shore, editor of the *Journal of Social Work & Human Sexuality*, wrote:

"There is no current validity to the hypothesis that the extent of exposure to erotica is positively associated with the immediate or later emergence of sexual pathology in general, and pedophilia in particular. My conclusions are consistent with those of Dr. Herant Katchadourian, the highly respected Stanford University physician who undertook a similar review of the literature for the fourth edition of his widely adopted textbook *Fundamentals of Human Sexuality*.... Moreover, child molesters were found to be essentially unmoved by such stimulation.... From a cross-cultural perspective, the Danish experience with the legalization of pornography and the Japanese experience with open aggressive erotica at the very least suggest that erotica does not increase the prevalence of sex crimes."

● In *The Question of Pornography: Research Findings and Policy Implications* (1987, New York, The Free Press, a division of Macmillan Inc., p. 172), Donnerstein, Linz and Penrod concluded:

"Should harsher penalties be leveled against persons who traffic in pornography, particularly violent pornography? We do not believe so. Rather, it is our opinion that the most prudent course of action would be the development of educational programs that would teach viewers to become more critical consumers of the mass media.... Educational programs and stricter obscenity laws are not mutually exclusive, but the legal course of action is more restrictive of personal freedoms than an educational approach. And, as we have noted, the existing research probably does not justify this approach."

● In his 1987 *Society* article on the Meese Commission, Dr. Larry Baron (Yale, University of New Hampshire) wrote:

"There is no empirical evidence to support the conclusion that nonviolent pornography increases aggression against women....

"A particularly insidious aspect of the *Final Report* is the commission's use of feminist rhetoric to attain its right-wing objectives. Replacing the outmoded cant of sin and depravity with the trendier rhetoric of harm, the commission exploited feminist outrage about sexual violence in order to bolster oppressive obscenity laws. The commission would have us believe that sexual aggression can be controlled through the strict regulation of obscene materials, an illusion that shifts our attention away from the structural sources of rape ... such issues as sexism, racism, poverty and a host of other factors ignored in the *Final Report*." ("Immoral, Inviolate or Inconclusive?", vol. 24 no. 5, p. 12)

● In their 1987 *American Psychologist* article on the Meese Commission, Linz, Donnerstein and Penrod again concluded:

"To single out pornography for more stringent legal action is inappropriate—based on the empirical research.... If the commissioners were looking for ways to curb the most nefarious media threat to the public, they missed it:" ("The Findings and Recommendations of the Attorney General's Commission on Pornography: Do the Psychological 'Facts' Fit the Political Fury?" vol. 42, no. 10)

● In 1990, Donnerstein and Linz reemphasized their findings in an overview of the literature prepared for the government of New Zealand. They wrote:

"Despite the Attorney General's Commission's assertion that most forms of pornography have a causal relationship to sexually aggressive behavior, we find it difficult to understand how this conclusion was reached.... Most social scientists who testified before the commission were also cautious, even when making statements about causal links between exposure to *violent* [emphasis original] pornography and sexually aggressive behavior. *Any reasonable review of the research literature would not come to the conclusion that ... pornography conclusively results in antisocial effects*." (emphasis added, p. 6)

1F. Commissions in Denmark, Canada and Britain conducted investigations on the effects of sexually explicit material.

In fact: The Danish, Canadian and British studies found no link between sexual material and social harm.

● In 1985, the Institute of Criminal Science at the University of Copenhagen reported that in European countries where restrictions on pornography have been lifted, incidence of rape over the last 10–20 years has declined or remained constant. (Berl Kutchinsky, *Society*, 1987, vol. 24, no. 10, p. 22)

• At the time of the Meese Commission, the Canadian Department of Justice completed its report on the effects of sexually explicit material, "Working Papers on Pornography and Prostitution, Report #13, The Impact of Pornography: An Analysis of Research and Summary of Findings" (known as the Fraser Committee Report). It found:

"There is no systematic research evidence available which suggests a causal relationship between pornography and morality.... There is no systematic research which suggests that increases in specific forms of deviant behavior, reflected in crime trend statistics (e.g., rape) are causally related to pornography." (p. 93)

"There is no persuasive evidence that the viewing of pornography causes harm to the average adult ... that exposure causes the average adult to harm others ... that exposure causes the average adult to alter established sex practices. On the contrary, the research supports the contention that exposure, although possible producing a short-term, transient alteration in patterns, has no effect in the longer term." (p. 94)

• The British Inquiry into Obscenity and Film Censorship (Williams Committee), 1979, in its report on pornography, also found no link between sexual imagery and social harms and rejected laboratory studies that attempted to equate aggression in controlled laboratory studies with violence in the real world.

The British commission wrote, "We unhesitatingly reject the suggestion that the available statistical information for England and Wales lends any support to the argument that pornography acts as a stimulus to the commission of sexual violence." (p. 80)

The Australian parliament's hearings concluded that sexually nonviolent and sexually violent material produces antisocial and violent effects.

In fact: Unlike the Meese Commission, the Surgeon General's conference and the Canadian Justice Department (Fraser) report, the Australian parliament commissioned no experts to read and evaluate the social science data.

• Donnerstein testified in *Her Majesty the Queen against Fringe Product Inc.* (1989):

"They should have had access and, it is my understanding, had access to all papers by the same group of researchers.... In the Meese Commission, you had members who were familiar with or who could evaluate social science data versus those who could not. Those who could, did file a minority report. The actual social science report reviewed and written by Edna Einsiedel did not support the [Meese Commission's] recommendations.... The Fraser [Canadian] Committee, it is my understanding, had a separate volume written by social scientists evaluating the social science research. That was not the case, it is my understanding, for the Australian parliament."

1G. Methodological issues in social science research

● In their writings, Drs. Neil Malamuth (University of California), David Shore (Southern Illinois University), Donnerstein, Linz et al. have noted that the Meese Commission failed to take into account certain important methodological problems that confound all social science data.

"Some commission members apparently did not understand or chose not to heed some of the fundamental assumptions in the social science research on pornography," wrote Donnerstein and Linz in *Psychology Today*. (December 1986, p. 56)

● Surgeon General Koop's conference on pornography devoted eight pages of its report to the methodological problems running through the scientific data. Chief among the data's limitations are:

(1) Results achieved in the experimental laboratory are notoriously bad predictors of behavior outside the lab. The Surgeon General's report concluded, "The drawback of such a [laboratory] approach is its inherent artificiality; phenomena in the lab are not always what they may be in the real world." (pp. 8, 9)

(2) Self-reporting questionnaires (such as questions about a lab subject's willingness to use force for sex) are poor indicators of real-life behavior. People exaggerate or minimize, and often don't do what they say they do.

(3) Experiments where subjects are asked to hurt a confederate "subject" are also poor predictors of real-life behavior as subjects are likely to know that in a lab setting, no scientist can or would allow a subject to be hurt.

In 1986, David Shore, editor of the *Journal of Social Work & Human Sexuality*, wrote, "Some recent works have suggested violence in pornography elevates aggression.... It should be noted that my research has lead to my concurring with Katchadourian that 'the experimental situations set up in these studies tend to be contrived, and the tests used artificial, (thus) their significance with respect to deviant behaviors remains uncertain.'"

(4) Researchers are inclined to interpret events according to their own beliefs, especially those reporting on clinical, in-the-field data.

"The most subtle problem with clinical reports," noted the Surgeon General's report, "is the inevitable tendency ... to interpret and report their observations in a way that supports their beliefs." (p. 8)

(5) Only successful studies are reported in the literature.

"As a result," wrote the Surgeon General's report, "it is difficult to know how many studies were done that were unable to produce any observed result.... The presence of a large number of these unreported results may indicate that the regularity and strength of a particular effect is really rather low even though it has been reported to have occurred under controlled conditions." (p. 10)

(6) Correlational data does not establish causality. For example, the number of drownings per day correlates highly with the sales of sunglasses, but it would be a mistake to say one causes the other. (p. 11)

(7) Clinical studies of convicted sex offenders cannot separate out their use of pornography from other highly significant factors that promote violence, such as drug or alcohol abuse, poverty, abusive childhoods, etc.

"Clinical studies are limited in value," wrote the Surgeon General's report. "Their greatest limitation is the inability to isolate the specific effects of the variable being considered (such as exposure to pornography) from other potentially influential variables." (p. 7)

(8) "Clinical studies have another problem resulting from their focus only on youth with identified problems. The effects of ... sexual abuse cannot be separated accurately from the effects of the discovery of those circumstances. For instance, it is impossible to tell with any rigor how much of the distress shown by a child in therapy results from actual participation in pornography and how much is precipitated by the reactions of others such as parents, friends and teachers to the discovery of the child's involvement. For example, Burgess et al. (1984) found that behavioral problems of some children involved in sex and pornography rings increased after their participation was discovered." (p. 7)

(9) The "desensitization" reported with repeated viewing of sexual material may be merely the usual boredom that results from repeatedly viewing any sort of material. Donnerstein pointed out during the Meese Commission that emergency room doctors don't faint at each new wounded body, yet that hardly means they will take to the streets and commit murder.

(10) Most of the research on pornography has been conducted on college men—a group especially vulnerable to the "sexual bravura" effect. Does a subject's knowledge that his answers will be compared to those of other college men skew his responses?

(11) All laboratory experiments are subject to the "experimenter demand" effect, where subjects try to guess (even unconsciously) at the experimenter's hypothesis and then to confirm it.

2. SEXUAL MATERIAL AND HARM

2A. Prevalence of violence in sexually explicit material

To arrive at its recommendations to restrict sexually explicit material, the Meese Commission concluded that (1) pornography has become more violent since the 1970 President's Commission on Obscenity and Pornography, which found no link between sexual material and antisocial behavior and recommended no restrictions; and that (2) pornographic images so significantly change men's attitudes about women that they promote and foster sexual assault.

In fact: The prevalence of violence in sexually explicit material since the 1970 President's Commission on Obscenity and Pornography has <u>decreased</u>.

• In their analysis of 4,644 "pornographic" magazines, the Meese Commission concluded that *Playboy, Penthouse* and *Playgirl* sorts of publications should not be considered pornographic. Dr. Jennings Bryant, whose research was heavily cited by the Meese Commission to condemn pornographic materials, classified *Penthouse, Playboy* and *Playgirl* as "R-rated softcore sexually oriented magazines." (Meese Commission Report, 1986)

• Dr. Joseph Scott and Steven Cuvelier (Ohio State University) ran a content analysis of *Playboy* over a 30-year period and found an average of 1.89 violent pictorials per year, with violence *decreasing* through the Eighties. ("Sexual Violence in *Playboy* Magazine: A Longitudinal Content Analysis," *Journal of Sex Research*, 1987, vol. 23, no. 4, pp. 534–539; "Violence in Playboy Magazine: A Longitudinal Analysis," *Archives of Sexual Behavior*, 1987, vol. 16, no. 4, pp. 279–287)

They wrote, "Although the overall number and ratio of violent cartoons and pictorials in *Playboy* over the 30-year period examined was rare, a major question addressed was whether the amount of violence was increasing. Rather than a linear relation, a curvilinear relationship was observed with the amount of violence on the decrease.... Those who argue for greater censorship of magazines such as *Playboy* because of its depictions of violence need a new rationale to justify their position." (*Archives of Sexual Behavior*, vol. 16, no. 4, p. 279)

In concluding their *Journal of Sex Research* article, Scott and Cuvelier wrote, "In the oldest continuously published adult magazine in the U.S., the number of sexually violent depictions has always been extremely small and the number of such depictions has decreased in recent years." (1987, p. 538)

• In his study of XXX video cassettes, Dr. Ted Palys of Simon Fraser University found a *decrease* in violence in sexually explicit videos. More violence was found in videos without explicit sexual activity than in the triple X, sexually explicit variety. ("Testing the Common Wisdom: The Social Content of Video Pornography," *Canadian Psychology*, 1986, vol. 27, pp. 22–35)

• Reviewing the literature on violence in sexually explicit material, Donnerstein and Linz wrote, "We cannot legitimately conclude that pornography has become more violent since the time of the 1970 Pornography Commission." (*Psychology Today*, December 1986, p. 57)

Linz, Donnerstein and Penrod repeated their findings in a 1987 *American Psychologist* article:

"We cannot legitimately conclude that the Attorney General's first assumption about pornography—that it has become increasingly more violent since the time of the 1970 Pornography Commission—is true.... The available data might suggest that there has actually been a decline in violent images within mainstream publications such as *Playboy* and that comparisons of X-rated materials with other depictions suggest there is in fact far more violence in the *non*pornographic fare." (vol. 42, no. 10)

• In a 1990 content analysis of current videos, Drs. Ni Yang and Daniel Linz (University of California) found that in explicit pornography, sexual behavior accounted for 41 percent of all behavioral sequences, sexual violence for 4.73 percent and nonsexual violence for another 4.73 percent. In R-rated tapes, sexual behavior accounted for 4.59 percent of behavioral sequences, sexual violence for 3.27 percent and nonsexual violence for 35 percent. ("Movie Ratings and the Content of Adult Videos: The Sex–Violence Ratio," *Journal of Communication*, 1990, vol. 40, no. 2, p. 34)

2B. Effects of exposure to nonviolent and "degrading" sexually explicit material (studies by Dolf Zillman, J.V.P. Check, and peer responses)

The Meese Commission held that exposure to sexual material—"normal" nonviolent and "degrading" (showing women in subordinate positions or in unusual sexual practices)—promotes and fosters sexual abuse.

In fact: Research data on nonviolent sexual images show no link between them and sexual aggression.

• Studies by Drs. Dolf Zillmann and Jennings Bryant (Indiana University) found that while long-term exposure to "degrading" pornography resulted in more calloused beliefs about rape in laboratory settings, long-term exposure also led to *less aggressive behavior*. ("Effects of Massive Exposure to Pornography," in *Pornography and Sexual Aggression*, 1984, New York, Academic Press; "Pornography, Sexual Callousness, and the Trivialization of Rape," *Journal of Communication*, 1982, vol. 32, pp. 10–21)

• At hearings before the New Zealand Indecent Publications Tribunal in 1990, Donnerstein said that any reasonable review of the research literature would *not* come to the conclusion that exposure to "degrading" pornography yields antisocial behavior. Donnerstein added:

"Specific depictions of the anal region do not seem to indicate any changes in specific attitudes about women or acceptability of violence against women." Donnerstein also said he "knew of no research which suggested that men with a sexual interest in adult women with shaved genitalia had therefore any interest in children."

• Additionally, several other studies over the last 20 years have shown that nonviolent pornography *reduces* aggression in laboratory settings. (D. Zillmann and B. Sapolsky, *Journal of Personality and Social Psychology*, 1977, vol. 35, pp. 587–596; R. Baron, *Journal of Personality and Social Psychology*,

1974, vol. 30 (3), pp. 318–322; R. Baron, *Human Aggression*, 1977, New York, Plenum Press; R. Baron and P. Bell, *Journal of Personality and Social Psychology*, 1977, vol. 35, pp. 79–87; N. Malamuth, "Erotica, Aggression and Perceived Appropriateness," paper presented at the 86th convention of the American Psychological Association, 1978; L. White, *Journal of Personality and Social Psychology*, 1979, vol. 37, pp. 591–601)

● Other researchers have not been able to replicate the component of Zillmann's 1982 study showing that "degrading" pornography promotes calloused perceptions of rape in laboratory subjects. In 1987, *American Psychologist* reported:

"Only one study has shown that long-term exposure to this type of [degrading] material changes an individual's perception of a rape victim (Zillmann & Bryant, 1982) [*Journal of Communication*, vol. 32, pp. 10–21]. But later studies with both male and female viewers have not replicated these findings (Krafka, 1985; Linz, 1985). [C. Krafka, "Sexually Explicit, Sexually Violent, and Violent Media: Effects of Multiple Naturalistic Exposures and Debriefing on Female Viewers," doctoral dissertation, University of Wisconsin; D. Linz, "Sexual Violence in the Media: Effects on Male Viewers and Implications for Society," doctoral dissertation, University of Wisconsin]

"Furthermore, only one study has found changes in subjects' willingness to say they would use force with a woman in order to have sex. This study, conducted by Check (1984) [J. V. P. Check, "The Effects of Violent and Nonviolent Pornography," for the Canadian Department of Justice, Ottawa, Ontario] involved several methodological procedures which prevent us from placing as much confidence in the outcome as we would like." (*American Psychologist*, 1987, vol. 42, no. 10)

Because of methodological flaws, the Canadian Department of Justice rejected the Check study.

● Surgeon General Koop's conference on pornography concluded that the only statement it could support regarding "degrading" sexual material was that exposure caused subjects to think a variety of sexual practices were more commonly practiced. Exposure caused subjects to estimate the prevalence of varied sexual practices *more accurately.* (Surgeon General's Report, p. 17)

● In his 1989 testimony to the District Court of Ontario (*Her Majesty the Queen against Fringe Product Inc.*), Donnerstein was asked, "As to the existence of negative effects arising from dehumanizing or degrading sexually explicit material, what is the bottom line on that?" Donnerstein said:

"There is too much conflicting data, too much controversy, too much methodological problems to make a statement.... I would have to lean, however ... that *there are no effects or if effects occur at all, just like with violent material, they can in fact occur ... outside the context of sexual explicitness.*" (emphasis added)

● The Meese Commission's report on the social science data, prepared by Dr. Edna Einsiedel (University of Calgary), concluded that the data on "degrading" pornography was too methodologically confused to use. (Meese Commission Report, 1986)

2C. Effects of exposure to nonviolent sexual materials and harm (studies by John Court, and peer responses)

Dr. John Court, professor of the Graduate School of Psychology at Fuller Seminary, Pasadena, California (formerly at Flinders University South Australia), reports finding a causal relationship between sexually explicit materials and sex crimes.

In fact: Court testified that there is no evidence of such a link.

● At the New Zealand Indecent Publications Tribunal in 1990, Court was asked, "Do you say that there is no causal link between nonviolent erotica and sexual crimes?"

He responded, "No, I don't say that.... What I am saying is that we do not have evidence that there is such a causal link. I cannot sustain it from my data and I don't know anybody who can."

● In their 1990 overview of the social science data prepared for the government of New Zealand, Donnerstein and Linz wrote:

"Studies in which individuals have been massively exposed to this [*Penthouse*] type of material have shown either reductions in laboratory aggression or *no increases* in aggressive behavior. Consequently, the conclusion that *nonviolent degrading materials* influence sexual aggression is *without support.*" (emphasis added, p. 41)

● In his November 1990 testimony to the New Zealand Indecent Publications Tribunal, Donnerstein commented on the idea that sexually explicit material could act as a trigger to sexual aggression.

He said that in his view, "the vast majority of studies indicated that no such trigger mechanism or capacity existed."

● Expressing similar views in his testimony to the Ontario District Court in *Her Majesty against Fringe Product Inc.* (1989), Donnerstein explained the impossibility of determining what will trigger someone to violence.

"Q.: Can you predict what phenomena will set these predisposed, already aggressive individuals off?

A.: I wish we could.... Certain people are influenced by who knows what. If you find a serial murderer and he's modeled something he sees, it could be any type of material. We know full well, with pedophiles, they are just as turned on by child pornography, which is obviously illegal, to a picture of a young male or female in the Sears catalog in underwear. It is very difficult to say what type of stimuli are going to take those individuals on the fringe, predisposed, and cause them to act in a certain way."

● In hearings before the New Zealand Indecent Publications Tribunal in 1990, Daniel Linz testified:
"With respect to case studies, it has not been established if the materials presented caused that person to be violent, or that an already violent individual is drawn to violent materials that reaffirm existing attitudes or predispositions. *In fact, many studies have found that following prolonged exposure to extremely sexually exciting stimuli, there are lowered levels of aggression,* and there is the corollary that the individual with less exposure actually behaves in a more violent fashion than the person with more exposure." (emphasis added)

2D. Effects of exposure to sexually explicit material on women's self-esteem

In fact: Research shows no lowering of women's self-esteem after exposure to sexually explicit materials.

● Dr. Carol Krafka found that women exposed even to sexually degrading materials did not engage in more sex role stereotyping, experience lower self-esteem, have less satisfaction with body image, hold more negative beliefs about rape or show greater acceptance of violence against women. ("Sexually Explicit, Sexually Violent, and Violent Media: Effects of Multiple Naturalistic Exposures and Debriefing on Female Viewers," 1985, doctoral dissertation, University of Wisconsin)

● Donnerstein came to similar results in a 1984 study, and Linz, Donnerstein and Penrod again in 1988. ("Pornography: Its Effect on Violence Against Women," in *Pornography and Sexual Aggression*, 1984, Orlando, Florida, Academic Press; Linz, Donnerstein and Penrod, "The Effects of Long-Term Exposure to Violent and Sexually Degrading Depictions of Women," *Journal of Personality and Social Psychology*, 1988, vol. 55, pp.758–768)

2E. Effects of exposure to sexually explicit material on social stability and the public good (studies by Dolf Zillman and Jennings Bryant, and peer responses)

Dolf Zillmann and Jennings Bryant found that exposure to pornography produced more acceptance of premarital and extramarital sexual relations, less satisfaction with one's sexual partner and less emphasis on marriage and having children.

In fact: The Surgeon General's conference reported that prolonged exposure to pornography led subjects to more accurately estimate the prevalence of varied sexual practices in the general public.

● Zillmann and Bryant presented their studies to the 1986 Surgeon General's conference on pornography. (Their work is found in "Effects of

Massive Exposure to Pornography," in *Pornography and Sexual Aggression*, 1984, New York, Academic Press; also in *Pornography: Research Advances and Policy Considerations*, 1989, Hillsdale, New Jersey, Erlbaum.)

The only statement regarding pornography and the social good that the Surgeon General's conference would endorse is that prolonged exposure to pornography increased subjects' estimation of the frequency of varied sexual practices. Subjects who had been in the intermediate- and massive-exposure groups in the Zillmann study estimated the prevalence of varied sexual practices in the general population *more accurately* than the control group. (Surgeon General's Report, p. 17)

• In their 1990 overview of the literature, Donnerstein and Linz ask, "What if these ideas had been presented in a nonsexually explicit format, would the effects have remained the same? [These ideas] are not endemic to pornography nor are they unavailable in other forms of mass media entertainment.... Findings such as those claimed by Zillmann and Bryant must remain tentative." (1990 report to the government of New Zealand, p. 33)

3. VIOLENT MATERIAL AND HARMS

3A. Effects of exposure to sexually violent material

The Meese Commission held that exposure to sexually violent imagery promotes and fosters sexual aggression.

In fact: The effects of sexually violent material is undecided in the scientific community. These effects can be measured only in laboratory settings and are not easily translated to life situations. Research indicates that negative effects attributed to sexually violent material stem from the violent, not the sexual, content.

• In 1978, Dr. Neil Malamuth (University of California) found that college-aged men in lab experiments showed increased aggression towards female confederate "subjects" after viewing sexually violent material if the men were told it was permissible to aggress against the women. When they were given no encouragement to aggress, they did not. ("The Sexual Responsiveness of College Students to Rape Depictions: Inhibitory and Disinhibitory Effects," *Journal of Personality and Social Psychology*, 1978, vol. 14, pp. 121–137)

• Through the 1980s, researchers such as Donnerstein, Linz, Dr. Leonard Berkowitz (University of Wisconsin) and Penrod found that exposure to violent material—sexual or *nonsexual*—increased aggression toward women in a lab context. (E. Donnerstein and L. Berkowitz, "Victim Reactions in Aggressive-Erotic Films as a Factor in Violence Against Women," *Journal of Personality and Social Psychology*, 1981, vol. 41, pp. 710–724; E. Donnerstein,

"Erotica and Human Aggression," in *Aggression: Theoretical and Empirical Reviews*, 1983, New York, Academic Press; E. Donnerstein, "Pornography: Its Effect on Violence Against Women," in *Pornography and Sexual Aggression*, 1984, Orlando, Florida, Academic Press; E. Donnerstein, D. Linz and S. Penrod, *The Question of Pornography: Research Findings and Policy Implications*, 1987, New York, The Free Press, a division of Macmillan Inc.)

• Commenting on the last decade of research, Donnerstein and Linz wrote that their findings "are accurate as long as we are referring to laboratory studies of aggression.... Whether this aggression is representative of real-world aggression, such as rape, is entirely different matter." (1990 report to the government of New Zealand, p. 37)

• In 1986, Malamuth and Dr. Joseph Ceniti (University of California) found no increase in aggression toward women in men who had watched sexually violent material. (*Aggressive Behavior*, 1986, vol. 12, pp. 129–137)

• Explaining the research on increases in (laboratory) aggression after viewing violent material, Donnerstein told the District Court of Ontario (1989):
"The measure is simply arousal, not sexual arousal. The Zillmann research strongly shows that once you get arousal up—the measures could be heart rate, galvanic skin response; blood pressure is the common one—*if arousal is high and subjects are aggressing, it's going to facilitate aggressive behavior, independent of where the arousal comes from. And yes, there are studies where males bicycle ride and then are more aggressive when they are angered.*" (emphasis added)
In sum, subjects in lab experiments will increase their aggression if they are angered. It they are "worked up" in any way, including from aerobic exercise, they will aggress more. This increase in aggression is not dependent on viewing sexual or violent material.

• After Surgeon General Koop's conference in 1986, N. Malamuth wrote a letter to *American Psychologist* to correct some misstatements published there about material that "portrays sexual aggression as pleasurable for the victim." He wrote:
"We [the Surgeon General's conference] did *not* reach the consensus that 'this type of pornography is at the root of much of the rape that occurs today.'... We also agreed that 'acceptance of coercive sexuality appears to be related to sexual aggression,' but we did *not* conclude that 'if a man sees a steady stream of sexually violent material ... he begins to believe that coercion and violence are acceptable ... and may himself become the perpetrator.'" (emphasis added)

• In their December 1986 *Psychology Today* article, Donnerstein and Linz wrote:

"The most callous attitudes about rape ... were found among those men who had seen only the violent coercion. Subjects who saw the X-rated version without violence scored the lowest." (p. 59)

● In 1989, Donnerstein testified to the District Court of Ontario:

"Research that has pitted the two against each other has demonstrated that it is the R-rated explicitly graphic violence but not sexually explicit material that is more potent in terms of [negative laboratory] effects than the highly sexually explicit material which would contain violence. That is endorsed, in very concrete terms, by the Meese Commission."

● In all lab studies where male subjects aggress against female confederate "subjects," the aggression is *non*sexual. (It is also fake, rigged to look like it is "hurting" the female confederates for the sake of the experiment.) Madeline Morris (Yale University) wrote:

"This finding has been interpreted by some to mean that violent pornography fosters sexual aggression against women. Such an interpretation is inappropriate since nonsexual aggression is not a valid indicator of sexual aggression." ("Governmental Regulation of Pornography: Rhetoric of Harm," paper to the American Sociological Association, 1985, p. 23)

3B. Sexually explicit material and addiction theory (Victor Cline and peer responses)

According to Mormon psychologist Victor Cline, pornography creates a cumulative effect that causes the viewer to need more and more hard-core or violent fare, which eventually leads to violent behavior.

In fact: Most social scientists do not consider Dr. Cline a reliable source of research information.

● Victor Cline to date has published no scholarly articles on sexual material. He has three articles on the effects of television violence on children in such popular publications as *Ladies' Home Journal* and *Life* magazine, and he has one article on the effects of television violence on children in a professional publication (*Journal of Personality and Social Psychology*, 1973, vol. 27, p. 360). He has edited one book, *Where Do You Draw The Line?*, (1974, Brigham Young University Press).

● Dr. Edna Einsiedel, in her review of the science for the Meese Commission, reported that there is no evidence that exposure to hard-core, violent or paraphiliac pornography creates an attraction to such material or stimulates a need for it. (Meese Commission Report, 1986)

● Dr. Elizabeth Allgeier, editor of the *Journal of Sex Research,* explained that Victor Cline has done no empirical studies. Without such research, scientists in the areas of psychology or sociology have no substantive material from Cline to evaluate or discuss. In the 1990 book *Sexual Interactions*, reviewing all scientific research in the field to date, the authors did not include or mention Victor Cline. (Allgeier and Allgeier, *Sexual Interactions*, third edition, 1990, D.C. Heath)

●In a 1984 lab experiment, D. Zillmann allowed male college students to chose to watch an X or XXX video. Many chose the XXX tapes, which included some paraphiliac material. In her review of the literature, Einsiedel called this choice "curiosity." There is no evidence in the Zillmann study, said Einsiedel, that the students liked the paraphilias or developed a taste for them. (Meese Commission Report, 1986)

●In their evaluation of the research on whether or not repeated exposure to sexually explicit material has cumulative effects, Donnerstein and Linz wrote that "the evidence ... points to the latter conclusion. This fact seems not to have been given sufficient consideration by the [Meese] Commission." (*Psychology Today*, December 1986, p. 57)

3C. Debriefings of laboratory subjects in studies on exposure to violent material, and implications for mitigating negative effects

●Based on the research of Malamuth and Check, Krafka, Donnerstein and Linz, the Surgeon General's report recommended a "media literacy program" to mitigate effects of media.

"Several studies have shown that presentations outlining the ways that violent sexual material can foster or reinforce incorrect beliefs or negative attitudes have been able to prevent the expected results of exposure. In other words, educating people about the possible effects of exposure, in conjunction with exposure, appears to reduce or eliminate the shifts in attitudes that are usually seen after exposure." (J. Check and N. Malamuth, "Can There Be Positive Effects of Participation in Pornography Experiments?" *Behaviour Research and Therapy*, 1984, vol. 22, pp. 535–548; N. Malamuth and J. Check, "Debriefing Effectiveness Following Exposure to Pornographic Rape Depictions," *Journal of Sex Research*, 1984, vol. 20, pp. 1–13; C. Krafka, "Sexually Explicit, Sexually Violent, and Violent Media: Effects of Multiple Naturalistic Exposures and Debriefing on Female Viewers," 1985, doctoral dissertation, University of Wisconsin; E. Donnerstein, "Techniques Designed to Mitigate the Impact of Mass Media Sexual Violence on Adolescents and Adults," paper presented to Surgeon General's Workshop on Pornography and Public Health, 1986; Report of the Surgeon General's Report, p. 50)

● Margaret Intons-Peterson, professor of psychology at Indiana University and former editor of the *Journal of Experimental Psychology*, found that if experimental subjects were given general information about male-female relationships or information on rape, showing those subjects sexually explicit or violent films had no effects on attitudes about rape and did not increase aggression toward women in the lab setting. (Intons-Peterson et al., "Will Educational Materials Offset Negative Effects of Violent Pornography?" 1987, Indiana University)

Donnerstein told the District Court of Ontario in 1989:

"Intons-Peterson did that, and she found that prebriefings on sex education or rape education mitigated the effects of seeing a sexually violent film or an R-rated film.... You didn't find subjects showing desensitization to these films and ... they weren't calloused about the rape victim."

● Continuing discussion of the research on briefing lab subjects about pornography, Donnerstein told the District Court of Ontario:

"We have also done it [mitigated lab effects of violent material] by having subjects video-tape themselves, write essays about rape and about the problems of mass media violence ... and you also get decreases. This, in conjunction with a vast amount of research with children and adolescents on intervention programs—the word is sometimes called critical viewing skills—suggests very strongly to the scientific community, as it did to our Surgeon General [Koop, 1986 conference on pornography] that these types of programs would be and could be incredibly effective as an intervention against exposure to all types of media."

●Donnerstein concluded in the Ontario District Court proceedings:

"If we could construct educational programs, prebriefing interventions, then it is my firm belief that we in fact could mitigate the negative impact of this type of material.... You don't do it right before the person sees it in the theater. You go ahead and make these educational programs for adolescents and children so that when they do in fact confront the material, they see it differently."

● Donnerstein, Linz and Penrod wrote in *American Psychologist*:

"Rather than call for stricter laws, we call for a more informed public.... The most prudent course of action would be the development of educational interventions which would teach viewers to become more critical consumers of the mass media." (1987, vol. 42, no. 10)

4. SEXUAL MATERIAL AND RAPE RATES

4A. Exposure to sexually explicit material and likelihood to rape (studies by Dolf Zillman and Jennings Bryant, and peer responses)

Dolf Zillmann and Jennings Bryant have reported that exposure to pornography in laboratory settings correlates positively with insensitivity to rape and rape victims.

In fact: The research shows that nonviolent sexual material does not affect subjects' likelihood to rape; though some studies of violent—not sexual—

material show decreasing sensitivity to rape, it remains difficult to translate this laboratory data to life situations.

• In 1986, Donnerstein, Linz and Berkowitz found that men report the harshest attitudes about rape after viewing violent films without any sexual content (*Psychology Today,* December 1986, p. 59):

"The most callous attitudes about rape ... were found among those men who had seen only the violent coercion. Subjects who saw the X-rated version without violence scored the lowest."

• In testimony to the Ontario District Court in 1989, Donnerstein said:

"After viewing a sexually explicit film, 11 percent of the male subjects said they would rape. For the aggressive pornography film, 25 percent said they would rape. For the [nonsexual] aggression-only film, 50 percent said they would rape."

Earlier, Donnerstein testified, "With sexually explicit violent depictions, the findings suggest increases in lab aggression, increases in certain—we can just call them callous—attitudes about certain myths about rape. *However, the caveat is you get those effects without any sexual content whatsoever. You get exactly the same effects just with the message about violence.*" (emphasis added)

• In a 1987 series of studies, Drs. V. Padgett and J. Brislin-Slutz found that exposure to nonviolent pornography—even if it was "degrading"— produced *no* decrease in men's sensitivity towards women and *no* increase in acceptance of the myth that women want to be raped or enjoy it. ("Pornography, Erotica and Negative Attitudes Towards Women: The Effects of Repeated Exposure," *Journal of Sex Research,* 1989, vol. 26, pp. 479–491)

It should be noted that Padgett employed a "power analysis"; that is, if the number of subjects were increased, would there be any effects from pornography? The conclusion was no.

• Donnerstein and Linz's 1990 overview of the social science literature prepared for the government of New Zealand reported,

"no effects for exposure [to *Penthouse*-type magazines] on antisocial attitudes such as less sensitivity to rape victims or greater endorsement of attitudes facilitating violence against women.... Most consistently, in long-term and short-term exposure studies, negative effects (e.g., lessened sensitivity toward rape victims, greater acceptance of force in sexual encounters) emerge when subjects are exposed to portrayals of overt violence against women or when sex is fused with aggression." (p. 4)

Donnerstein and Linz continued, "Studies in which individuals have been massively exposed to this [*Penthouse*] type of material have shown either *reductions* in laboratory aggression or no increases in aggressive behavior. Consequently, the conclusion that *nonviolent degrading materials* influence sexual aggression is *without support.*" (emphasis added, p. 41)

4B. The J.B. Weaver study on exposure to pornography and desensitivity to sexual violence

The J. B. Weaver study (1987) reports that pornography desensitizes men to rape and makes them accept sexual violence.

In fact: the Weaver study did not use pornography in its research protocol and leading researchers dispute its findings.

● Donnerstein pointed out to the Ontario District Court in 1989 that the Weaver study (doctoral dissertation, Indiana University) used no pornography and no X-rated material. It was based on material from popular television programs and movies.

● In a *Journal of Sex Research* review of Weaver's research, Linz dismissed all the findings of the Weaver study, saying Weaver's own statistical data do not support the claim that sexually explicit material changes attitudes about rape.

●Donnerstein told the Ontario District Court:
"He [Linz] says ... absolutely nothing is occurring and that no methodologist or qualified statistician could argue for effects. I would rather, in fact, say there are effects. In fact, I would be willing to give Weaver the benefit of the doubt and say there are many effects. *The problem is they have nothing to do with pornography.*" (emphasis added)

4C. Current incidence of rape

Increased reporting of rapes to the police suggests that the incidence of rape has been rising in recent years.

In fact: the increase in rape reporting to the police may reflect an increase in reporting only, and not an increase in the incidence of rape.

● The Bureau of Justice Statistics reports that the national rape rate of 0.6 per 1,000 remained steady between 1973 and 1987. Attempted rape rates have decreased 46 percent from 1.3 to 0.7 per 1,000 over the same period.
These statistics were gathered from household surveys rather than from police reports, where rapes are likely underreported. The Bureau of Justice Statistics data identify the many rapes that never reach police files because women are afraid to report them (especially in cases of domestic rape) or suspect the police won't do anything.
Additionally, these data cover the decades when feminists brought rape to the attention of the nation and created the social climate and structures— hotlines, special police department task forces and the like—to encourage women to bring rape into the open. This has lead to an overall increase in rape reporting. One would expect rape rates to increase, not to remain steady or decrease as is reported here.

4D. Correlation between rape rates and sales of sexually explicit material (studies by Larry Baron and Murry Strauss, Cynthia Gentry, and Joseph Scott and Loretta Schwalm)

In their 1984 study, Drs. Larry Baron and Murray Straus (Yale, University of New Hampshire) found a positive correlation between pornography circulation and rape rates.

In fact: Baron, Straus and others found this correlation to be spurious; it appears because both rape rates and pornography sales correlate with other factors, such as the number of young men living in a given locale and the presence of a macho ethic in that area.

● When Baron and Straus introduced into their data the Violence Approval Index—a "hypermasculinity" rating—the relationship between pornography circulation and rape disappeared. ("Sexual Stratification, Pornography, and Rape in the United States," in *Pornography and Sexual Aggression*, 1984, Orlando, Florida, Academic Press, pp. 185–209; Yale University, 1985, 1986)

● Baron explained at the Meese Commission hearings that "the relationship ... may be due to an unspecified third variable. It is quite plausible that the findings could reflect state-to-state differences in a hypermasculated or macho culture pattern." (For an overview of the Baron and Straus studies, see L. Baron and M. Straus, *Four Theories of Rape in American Society: A State-level Analysis*, 1989, New Haven, Connecticut, Yale University Press.)

● In Baron and Straus (1984, 1985, 1986), the correlations between sexual material and rape—even without the inclusion of the hypermasculinity rating—is far from conclusive: Utah ranks lowest on the Sexual Magazine Circulation Index but 25th in number of rapes; New Hampshire ranks ninth on the circulation index and 44th in rapes. ("Sexual Stratification, Pornography, and Rape in the United States," in *Pornography and Sexual Aggression*, 1984, Orlando, Florida, Academic Press, pp. 185–209; Yale University, 1985, 1986)

●In later studies, the correlation between rape rates and sexual materials sales disappeared when the number of young men living in a given area was factored into the data.

"There is no evidence of a relationship between popular sex magazines and violence against women," wrote Dr. Cynthia Gentry (Wake Forest University) in her 1989 study reviewing the data on the relationship between sexually explicit materials and rape.

The only factor that predicted the rape rate in a given locale was the number of men between the ages of 18 and 34 residing there. ("Pornography and Rape: An Empirical Analysis," *Deviant Behavior*, 1991, vol. 12, pp. 227–238)

● In 1988, Dr. Joseph Scott and Loretta Schwalm (Ohio State University) reported similar findings from their correlation studies. ("Rape Rates and the Circulation Rates of Adult Magazines," *Journal of Sex Research*, 1988, vol. 24, pp. 241–250)

● Also in 1988, Scott and Schwalm reported no correlation between the presence of adult theaters and rape rates. Other factors, such as the circulation of "outdoor-type" magazines, such as *Field & Stream, Guns and Ammo* and *The American Hunter*, correlated more closely with rape rates. ("Pornography and Rape: An Examination of Adult Theater Rates and Rape Rates by State," in *Controversial Issues in Crime and Justice*, 1988, Beverly Hills, California, Sage)

● In 1990, Dr. Larry Baron examined the degree of gender equality in a given area and the circulation rates of popular sexually oriented magazines (*Chic, Club, Gallery, Genesis, Hustler, Oui, Playboy* and *Penthouse*). He found that areas with *higher circulation rates show more gender equality*, and suggested that both sexually explicit material and gender equality may flourish in politically tolerant areas where there are fewer restrictions on speech.

The best predictor, in the Baron study, of gender inequality, was the number of fundamentalist religious groups in a given area. ("Pornography and Gender Equality: An Empirical Analysis," *Journal of Sex Research*, 1990, vol. 27, pp. 363–380)

4E. Cross-cultural studies of rape rates and the availability of sexually explicit material (studies by John Court, Berl Kutchinsky, and peer responses)

Dr. John Court (Graduate School of Psychology, Fuller Seminary, Pasadena, California, formerly at Flinders University South Australia) analyzed rape rates in Hawaii during a two-year period when sexual material was restricted there, and reported that rape rates decreased.

In fact: Leading scientists have repudiated Dr. Court's data; cross-cultural research indicates that the availability of pornography does not affect rape rates.

● The British Inquiry into Obscenity and Film Censorship (Williams Committee) read Court's work and rejected it:

"We unhesitatingly reject the suggestion that the available statistical information for England and Wales lends any support at all to the argument that pornography acts as a stimulus to the commission of sexual violence." (p. 80)

● In *Society*, Dr. Augustine Brannigan, University of Calgary, wrote:

"John Court, a self-proclaimed Christian psychologist and onetime leader of the antipornography Festival of Light, published a series of papers to discredit Kutchinsky's Danish study. The Williams Committee in the United Kingdom scrutinized his work and characterized it as misleading and intellectually dishonest." (1987, vol. 24, no. 5, p. 15)

• In the 1990 hearings by the New Zealand Indecent Publications Tribunal, Court was asked, "Do you say that there is no causal link between nonviolent erotica and sexual crimes?"

He responded, "No, I don't say that.... what I am saying is that we do not have evidence that there is such a causal link. I cannot sustain it from my data and I don't know anybody who can."

●According to Court's own data, Singapore, with tight controls on pornography, showed a much greater increase in rape rates (28 percentage points more) between 1964 and 1974 than did Stockholm, with liberalized pornography laws. Japan, with some of the world's most violent pornography, saw a 45 percent drop in rape rates for the same decade. (in *The Question of Pornography: Research Findings and Policy Implications*, 1987, New York, The Free Press, p. 64)

●Drs. P. Abramson and H. Hayashi report that Japan allows far greater nudity on television and in general-circulation magazines, and Japanese pornography much more frequently relies on themes of bondage and rape. Yet Japan reports a 2.4 rape rate per 100,000 people, compared with 34.5 in the U.S. ("Pornography in Japan: Cross-cultural and Theoretical Considerations," in *Pornography and Sexual Aggression*, 1984, Orlando, Florida, Academic Press)

●Denmark lifted restrictions on sexually explicit material in the mid-sixties and saw a decrease in sex crimes in the years since legalization. The rate of rape, in particular, did not increase with increased distribution of pornography but remained constant. (*The Question of Pornography: Research Findings and Policy Implications*, 1987, New York, The Free Press, a division of Macmillan Inc., pp. 61, 62)

• According to a 20-year study by Dr. Berl Kutchinsky, Institute of Criminal Science, University of Copenhagen, sex crimes against female children dropped from 30 per 100,000 to approximately 5 per 100,000 between 1965 and 1982. ("Pornography and Its Effects in Denmark and the United States: A Rejoinder & Beyond," in *Comparative Social Research: An Annual*, 1985)

• "Not only is there is possibly a direct causal link between pornography and the decrease in certain types of sex crimes," wrote Kutchinsky in Society, "but also and more importantly, sex crimes in Denmark, including rape, did not increase—as advocates of censorship had expected—despite the appearance and subsequent legalization of hard-core pornography." (1987, vol. 24, no. 5, p. 22)

• Continuing in the *Society* article, Kutchinsky wrote, "Since it was clear from the onset that most offenses involving homosexuality and prostitution have no obvious victims ... the detailed analysis of the decrease was restricted to 'regular' heterosexual sex crimes, that is, sex crimes committed by a male offender against a female (adult or child) victim. In Copenhagen ... these crimes constituted 85 percent of all sexual offenses and had an overall drop from 96 reported cases per 100,000 population in 1966 to 25 per 100,000 in 1973." (p. 22)

• Responding to Court's claims that rape rates in Denmark increased after legalization, Kutchinsky wrote:

"The fact is that rape in Copenhagen has neither increased nor decreased during the years when pornography became increasingly available. This fact is seen clearly in the next table, *which shows a case of scientific fraud by Mr. Court. This case is so clear that it would stand up in any court of justice.*" (emphasis added, Kutchinsky correspondence with Burton Joseph, attorney for *Playboy* magazine)

• In West Germany, rape rates declined slightly since bans on pornography were lifted in 1973, though there has been a rise in almost every other sort of violent crime.

"It is interesting," wrote Kutchinksy, "that Court and others who are interested in the effects of pornography on rape have never been interested in what happened in West Germany.... I am aware that rape also decreased in Italy (where pornography is very easily available) and that most of the European countries have unchanged rape levels." (Kutchinsky correspondence with B. Joseph, attorney for *Playboy* magazine)

5. SEXUAL MATERIAL AND PARAPHILIAS

5A. Role of sexually explicit material in the development of uncommon sexual practices, including pedophilia

In fact: research on unusual or violent sexual practices indicates they are not caused by exposure to sexual material but by early childhood emotional and/or physical abuse.

• Dr. Park Dietz, a Meese Commission member and professor of law and behavioral medicine and medical director of the Institute of Law, Psychiatry and Public Policy at the University of Virginia, said:

"No sprinkling of images, however deviant, can render an otherwise normal man either paraphiliac or criminal. The leap from fantasy to action has much to do with character and the vicissitudes of life and little or nothing to do with the objects of desire."

• The world's foremost researcher in this area, Dr. John Money of Johns Hopkins University, told *The New York Times* (January 23, 1990) that "he and other researchers found no evidence that pornography causes or fosters paraphilias (sexual abnormalities).... The majority of patients with paraphilias ... described a strict antisexual upbringing in which sex was either never mentioned or was actively repressed or defiled."

Money predicted that "current repressive attitudes toward sex will breed an ever-widening epidemic of aberrant sexual behavior."

●In the *American Journal of Psychotherapy* (1984, vol. 38, no. 2, p. 175), Money writes:

"The fantasies of paraphilia are not socially contagious. They are not preferences borrowed from movies, books or other people. They are not voluntary choices. They cannot be controlled by will power. Punishment does not prevent them, and persecution does not eradicate them, but feeds them and strengthens them."

●Drs. William Fisher (University of Western Ontario) and Donn Byrne (State University of New York at Albany) found that individuals with a history of restrictive sexual socialization had a more negative verbal and emotional response to pornography while being more affected by it in their behavior. ("Sex Differences in Response to Erotica? Love Versus Lust," *Journal of Personality and Social Psychology*, 1978, vol. 36, pp. 117–125)

●In his book *Vandalized Lovemaps* (with Dr. Margaret Lamacz, 1989, Prometheus Books), Money writes that normal sexual development is derailed in early childhood by such traumas as incest, physical abuse, neglect or emotional indifference, not sexually explicit material. Later, he paraphrased to *The New York Times* (January 23, 1990) that "a person with a particular pattern of erotic arousal seeks out pornographic material that 'turns him on' because it meshes with that pattern."

He earlier told the Meese Commission that the pornography industry has been "testing the size of the paraphiliac market" for 25 years, including "the purchasing power of those interests in violent and sadistic pornography," but they "are all appealing to a specialty market and not to people with normal sexual imagery."

●At hearings regarding the Department of Justice grant to Judith Reisman (to investigate her claims of child pornography in *Playboy, Penthouse* and *Hustler* magazines), FBI agent Ken Lanning said that child pornography appeals only to pedophiles—to men who are already aroused by such activity—and has "absolutely nothing to do with adult pornography.... If there were no pedophiles, there would be no child pornography—it has no other use."

Since the *Ferber* decision (1982), Lanning continued, child pornography has been "driven underground and is not openly sold anywhere in the U.S."

●In testimony to the Meese Commission, Dr. Richard Green (University of California), editor of *Archives of Sexual Behavior* for 20 years and the author of *The "Sissy Boy Syndrome" and the Development of Homosexuality*, said:

"We really don't know where some really unusual sexual behaviors come from. But the evidence that they come from an immediate linking during adolescent adulthood, with what would have been a neutral stimulus, doesn't seem to hold up."

Green also noted that "patterns of interest in erotic materials *followed* the emergence of sexual orientation."

●Dr. Gene Abel, professor of psychiatry at Emory University School of Medicine with an expertise in the field of sexual deviance, said:

"When we have done scientific studies of sex offenders, we have not found a relationship between the use of pornography and the commission of crimes or the use of aggression. Sex offenders have specific sexual interests, and then they seek out pornography that will match that. It isn't the other way around. They don't see the pornography and then develop the deviant interest."

●The Kinsey Institute study of 1,356 men convicted of sex crimes found that they were less responsive to and less interested in pornography than prisoners convicted of nonsexual crimes or men in the general population. (Gebhard et al., *Sex Offenders*, 1965, New York, Harper & Row)

●Dr. Michael Goldstein et al. found that for rapists and child molesters, exposure to pornography during both adolescence and adulthood was less than for the general public. They also found that rapists were more likely to come from home environments in which education about sexuality was very limited and attitudes towards sex were restrictive. (*Pornography and Sexual Deviance*, 1973, Los Angeles, University of California Press)

● In the *Harvard Civil Rights–Civil Liberties Law Review* (vol. 21, p. 70), Barry Lynn, former legislative counsel to the American Civil Liberties Union, wrote:

"While exposure to sexually explicit depictions of oral sex may increase the chances that a couple will try it, the same cannot be said for sex with chickens, coprophilia or actual sadism. As noted by many therapists, paraphilias will not spread broadly throughout the population as a result of people looking at pictures of them."

● Donnerstein told the Ontario District Court in 1989:

"We know full well, with pedophiles, that they are just as turned on by child pornography, which is obviously illegal, to a picture of a young male or female in the Sears catalog. It is very difficult to say what type of stimuli are going to take those individuals on the fringe, predisposed, and cause them to act....

"The most interesting thing about all the research is that it tends to indicate that for the other 99.99 percent, if we as parents sit down with those children and talk about violence on television, and talk about objectification in films, we actually mitigate the effect."

●In a prepared statement to Congress, John Money explained that pornography may have a cathartic effect on sex-offender patients. He wrote:

"Patients who request treatment in a sex-offender clinic commonly disclose that pornography helps them contain their abnormal sexuality within imagination only, as a fantasy, instead of having to act it out in real life with an unconsenting, resentful partner, or by force." (Congressional Hearings, 1970, note 14, 342)

●The Canadian Department of Justice report on pornography concluded:

"Although the specific contribution is not completely understood, there is some evidence to suggest that the controlled use of pornography can be of benefit as a therapeutic tool in the treatment of select clinical populations (e.g., incarcerated sexual offenders)." (*Working Paper on Pornography and Prostitution, Report #13, The Impact of Pornography: An Analysis of Research and Summary of Findings,* 1984, p. 95)

● In a 1990 report, prison officials at the Palm Beach, Florida, County Jail reported that prison fights had significantly decreased since the in-prison showing of popular "slasher" films. Between April and October 1986, prison officials broke up 522 fights. A month later, November 1986, the jail began showing films such as *The Texas Chainsaw Massacre Part 2* as part of its daily videotape screenings. Between April and October 1987, prison officials broke up 240 fights—more than a 50 percent decrease since the year before. Between January and July 1990, 188 fights occurred, almost a 25 percent decrease. (Cox News Service, 1990)

6. FBI AND POLICE DATA

6A. FBI study on the role of sexually explicit material in serial killings

According to the American Family Association, the FBI found that sexually explicit material plays a significant role in serial killings.

In fact: the FBI report on serial killings claimed no link between them and sexually explicit material.

●In 1989, the FBI told reporter Philip Nobile, "The FBI knows nothing about pornography." Its study on serial killers contains two sentences on it.

Dr. Ann Burgess, one of the authors of the FBI study on violent criminals explained that the FBI wasn't "looking at pornography. We didn't ask how often they thought about it. We never quantified it. We didn't ask them at what age they saw it."

●The Department of Justice rejected the FBI report for unacceptable methodology and statistics.

6B. Findings of the Michigan State Police on the role of sexually explicit material in sex crimes.

According to the American Family Association fact sheet "Boycott 'Lil Champ," columnist Jack Anderson reported that the Michigan police found that pornography is used or imitated in 41 percent of the sex crimes they investigate.

In fact: the Michigan State Police never conducted such a study and does not believe that sexually explicit material is the prime source of sex crimes.

● According to Detective Sergeant David Minzey, criminal profiler for the Michigan State Police, the Michigan police made no such study and claim no such findings.

Michigan has the oldest sex-motivated crime data base in the country, dating to the 1950s, with 70,000 cases recorded. Minzey's department has found no causal link between sexually explicit material and sex crimes. "We have gone into our data base," Minzey said, "and have never been able to pull out such a causal relationship."

The 41 percent statistic, Minzey explained, apparently comes from a master thesis by Darrell Pope at Michigan State University (1977). "There is a strong religious strain in Pope's work," Minzey said. "Pope was trying to establish causality, but as you know, you cannot establish causality between sexually explicit materials and sex crimes. We'd make a better causality case for alcohol.

"Our name got attached to the study about ten years ago—I don't know why. We keep getting inquiries about it. Please tell everybody that we did no such study," Minzey concluded. "We're tired of getting these calls." (interview with Detective Sergeant Minzey, April 12, 1991)

7. THE MEDIA AND MINORS

7A. Incidence of child abuse

Media attention to child abuse has led to the belief that child abuse has been increasing in recent years.

In fact: increases in the reporting of child abuse may reflect an increase of reporting only and not an increase in child abuse.

● The July 1991 issue of *Pediatrics* reported that child abuse "appears to have remained steady at about 12 percent for females over the last four decades." These statistics were gathered from personal surveys rather than from police files, where until very recently child abuse was significantly underreported. Recent increases in child abuse reporting is attributed, in *Pediatrics,* to the legal requirement to report child abuse and to attitudinal changes toward women and children rather than to an increase in child abuse.

7B. Presence of minors in sexually explicit material (study by Judith Reisman and peer responses)

In 1984, Judith Reisman was given $734,371 (nearly half again as much as the budget of the Meese Commission) by the U.S. Department of Justice to investigate her hypothesis that mainstream sexual material such as Playboy, Penthouse *and* Hustler *promotes child sexual abuse. She reported that between 1954 and 1984, those three publications printed 6,004 photographs, illustrations and cartoons depicting children—*Hustler, *14.1 times per issue;* Playboy, *8.2 times per issue;* Penthouse, *6.4 times per issue.*

In fact: Reisman's findings have been repudiated by most social science researchers, including those who commissioned her study.

●On April 11, 1984, Gordon Raley (staff director of the Human Resources Subcommittee of the Education and Labor Committee) called the Reisman grant "an unbelievable waste of taxpayers' dollars.... I have never seen a grant as bad as this, nor an application as irresponsibly prepared.... Our examination so far further indicates Ms. Reisman's credentials as a scientist are pretty flimsy."

●When Reisman delivered her final report, Reagan appointee Alfred Regnery, who had commissioned the study, said, "Bad judgments were exercised when the grant was first made."

● Regnery's successor, Verne Speirs, said the Department of Justice was shelving the report because of "multiple serious flaws in its methodology.... We have made a decision not to officially publish or disseminate the report."

●The American University, which provided the academic housing for Reisman's study, also refused to publish it.

●An independent academic auditor of the Reisman report, Dr. Robert Figlio (University of Pennsylvania), told American University:
"This manuscript cannot stand as a publishable and/or releasable product.... This project, the data gathered and the analyses undertaken offer no information about the effects that pornography and media may have on behavior.... The term child used in the aggregate sense in this report is so inclusive and general as to be almost meaningless.... From a scientific point of view, we cannot take this work seriously to build theory or policy."
To the press, Figlio said, "I wondered what kind of mind would consider the love scene from *Romeo and Juliet* to be child porn."

●At hearings regarding the Reisman grant, FBI agent Ken Lanning said that child pornography appeals only to pedophiles—to men who are already aroused by such activity—and it has "absolutely nothing to do with adult pornography.... If there were no pedophiles, there would be no child pornography—it has no other use."

Since the *Ferber* decision (1982), Lanning continued, child pornography has been "driven underground and is not openly sold anywhere in the U.S."

●Dr. Loretta Haroian, cochair of the plenary session on Child and Adolescent Sexuality at the 1984 World Congress of Sexology and one of the world's experts on childhood sexuality, said of the Reisman study:

"This is not science, it's vigilantism: paranoid, pseudoscientific hyperbole with a thinly veiled hidden agenda. This kind of thing doesn't help children at all.... Her [Reisman's] study demonstrates gross negligence and, while she seems to have spent a lot of time collecting data, her conclusions, based on the data, are completely unwarranted. The experts Reisman cites are, in fact, not experts at all but simply people who have chosen to adopt some misinformed, Disneyland conception of childhood that she has. These people are little more than censors hiding behind Christ and children."

●Dr. James Weinrich, a psychobiologist and author of *Sexual Landscapes*, whose research was given the Hugo Beigel Award in 1987 for the best work published in *The Journal of Sex Research*, said:

"Reisman utilizes some actual scientific principles ... but then turns around and goes off into her own lunacy.... Reisman's statements are spooky, meticulous in their way but often unprincipled and possibly crazy."

●In testimony before the New Zealand Indecent Publications Tribunal, Daniel Linz commented on Reisman's content analysis of *Penthouse* magazine. After listing several methodological problems, including "coder bias" (Reisman used seven of her regular employees, who are familiar with her views, to code depictions in *Playboy, Penthouse* and *Hustler* for violence or presence of minors), Linz concluded:

"The report presumes a view of human information processing which is now discredited. What humans do is organize material within context. This report presumes that the basis of information processing is that of a completely reactive individual who just responds to stimuli."

●Dr. Henry Giarretto, founder and executive director of The Child Sexual Abuse Treatment Program in Santa Clara, California, the oldest such program and model for others around the country, said:

"Our program has not been designed to include collection of data on the use of pornography because the literature and our own clinical experience showed no link between the commission of child sexual abuse and sexually explicit material. While it has been clinically noted that some perpetrators read and/or view sexually explicit material, many others express their feeling that pornography is immoral. In contrast to common belief, a great number of men who turn to their children for sexual purposes are highly religious or morally rigid individuals who feel that this is 'less of a sin' than masturbation or seeking sexual liaisons in an outside affair." (statement from the Child Sexual Abuse Treatment Program, April 1991)

7C. Effects of media on minors

●Dr. Beverly Lynch, former president of the American Library Association (ALA), testified before the Meese Commission:

"The American Library Association opposes restricted access to material and services for minors, and holds that it is *parents*—and only parents—who may restrict their children—*and only their children*—from access to library materials. We not only defend the right of parents to supervise and guide the reading habits of their children, but we assert that it is their responsibility."

It is the ALA's position not only that it is the responsibility of parents to guide the reading and viewing of their children but that most parents would rather do so—about sex, religion, politics, money and most other aspects of life. It is ALA's position that most parents would prefer not to have those decisions made for them by state authorities or other parents, however well-meaning.

The great difficulty in trying to restrict material that some parents believe is offensive is that adults hardly agree on the materials suitable for minors of different ages. One parent's literature, popular entertainment or music is another parent's trash. Some parents would encourage their minor children to see *Married ... with Children* or *The Last Tango in Paris* while others would prohibit them from reading *The Diary of Anne Frank*. One only need think of the debate over sex and AIDS education classes or of the controversy that began in 1990 over the *Impression* reading series. What some teachers and parents consider a syllabus that sparks students' interest in reading others believe contravenes their religious beliefs. The series' section on Halloween, which includes ghost and goblin stories, has been attacked for teaching witchcraft. At least two suits against school districts using the series were filed in Willard, Ohio, and Sacramento, California.

Should some parents be successful in eliminating the materials they believe are harmful to minors by removing them from libraries, stores or TV, they would keep those materials from other adults and other people's children—a determination most Americans would rather make themselves.

7C. Media and Minors: Effects of rock and roll on minors

●Testifying to the Ontario District Court, in 1989, Donnerstein reviewed the scientific literature on effects of rock and rock videos on minors.

"There has been research done ... on rock videos—rock videos that would contain violence and rock videos, for instance, that would contain sexist types of messages, and the findings are, again, absolutely nothing happens."

●In their 1986 study, Drs. Jill Rosenbaum and Lorraine Prinksy (California State University) found that, of over 600 songs, teenagers considered only a very few of them (7 percent) to be about sex, violence, drugs or the devil. For this subset of songs, the teenagers had a very limited understanding of the meaning of the lyrics and, most importantly, Rosenbaum and Prinsky note that teenagers' readings of songs differ substantially from those of adults, especially of adults who are most concerned about the effects of rock lyrics. ("'Leer-ics' or Lyrics: Teenage Impressions of Rock and Roll," *Youth and Society,* 1987, vol. 18, pp. 385–397)

They wrote, "The major objections to current popular music point to references of sex, violence, drugs and satanism. If youths are influenced by such themes, we would expect them to describe such topics in their favorite songs. However, these data indicate that the students hear or understand very little of the references to these topics." ("Sex, Violence and Rock 'n' Roll," *Popular Music and Society,* 1987, vol. 11, pp. 79–90)

●In a June 1991 article, *The New York Times* rock critic Jon Pareles examined two videotapes that attribute social harms to MTV. The first, called *Rising to the Challenge,* is sold by the Parents' Music Resource Center (PMRC), the group founded by Tipper Gore that persuaded record companies to put warning labels on their product. It was written by former PMRC executive director Jennifer Norwood and Robert DeMoss, youth-culture specialist for Focus on the Family, a Christian fundamentalist group. The second tape, called *Dreamworlds,* was made by Sut Jhally, professor of communications at the University of Massachusetts, and is being sold for classroom use.

Pareles discovered, upon investigating *Rising to the Challenge,* that the violent incidents that it claims were inspired by rock videos actually occurred before most of the albums mentioned were released, "suggesting," noted Pareles, "that the music reflects the culture instead of driving it." On examining *Dreamworlds,* Pareles found that the images of women were ripped out of context without indicating what proportion they form of all music-video images or even what videos they come from. In actual MTV, viewed in full and in context, Pareles found about one in six clips has "ornamental" or "sexy" women and "two minutes per hour of female bimbofication, along with such various nonbimbos as moms, teachers, old women and children" and, of course, female singers and bands.

Pareles concludes with this observation: "When a teenager sees some guy with waist-length two-tone hair, wearing leopard-print spandex and studded leather standing in a spotlight holding a guitar, he or she can probably figure out that it's a performance, a show, a fantasy—part of a privileged arena far away from daily life. Given the evidence, I wish I could say the same about their elders." (*The New York Times,* June 2, 1991)

7C. Media and Minors: Effects of exposure to sexually explicit language on minors

(Because of the ethical problems involved in showing minors sexual or violent imagery, the research below is scant and relies mainly on television programming.)

●The Surgeon General's report on pornography (1986) found that sexually explicit materials have little impact on children at an age when they do not have the cognitive capabilities to comprehend them.

"As children mature they develop new cognitive and emotional skills, and their interests shift. As a result of these changes in basic understanding and orientations, the message that an 8- or 12- or 16-year-old would get from a certain pornographic movie may be quite different from that of an 18-year-old.... Growing up in the 1980s is different than [sic] growing up in the 1960s, and sociohistorical changes can affect the rates of many things from juvenile crime to views of interpersonal relationships." (p. 36)

The report adds, "Speculating about the effects on children less than 12 years of age is even more of a problem. Younger children think in a qualitatively different manner from those on whom research regarding the effects of pornography are done.... The fear of some is that the sexual and emotional patterns to be followed by their children when they are grown will be 'imprinted' on them by seeing pornography at a younger age. Others believe that young children are less affected since they do not have the cognitive or emotional capacities needed to comprehend the messages of much pornographic material.... In the end, then, it is really rather difficult to say much definitively about the possible effects of exposure to pornography on children." (pp. 37–38)

The Surgeon General's report also noted, "Children bring individual temperaments and adaptive skills to situations, and the predictability of how particular influences will affect a child is lower than we might expect." (p. 38)

●In their 1990 overview of the research literature for the government of New Zealand, Donnerstein and Linz found:

"Even if exposed to sexual terms and innuendo, children under the age of 12 may not understand them. If children do not understand basic sexual concepts, it is unlikely that any indecent language referring to these sexual activities will be fully understood. Without such a understanding, it is difficult to see how these material could have a negative impact." (p. 45)

●In her 1989 book *Understanding Human Sexuality* (New York, McGraw Hill), Janet Hyde reported that American children between the ages of five and 15 are "sexual illiterates." (p. 646)

●In their book *Children's Sexual Thinking* (1982, London, Routledge & Kegan Paul), Ronald Goldman and Juliette Goldman reported that none of the nine-year-olds in their study knew the term uterus.

● These findings on sexual literacy are especially interesting in light of the repeated calls by researchers such as Donnerstein, Linz, Peterson and Krafka for increased and improved sex education in the U.S.

Donnerstein, Linz and Penrod wrote in their book *The Question of Pornography: Research Findings and Policy Implications* (1987, The Free Press, a division of Macmillan Inc., p. 172):

"Should harsher penalties be leveled against persons who traffic in pornography, particularly violent pornography? We do no believe so. Rather, it is our opinion that the most prudent course of action would be the development of educational programs that would teach viewers to become more critical consumers of the mass media.... Educational programs and stricter obscenity laws are not mutually exclusive, but the legal course of action is more restrictive of personal freedoms than an educational approach. And, as we have noted, the existing research probably does not justify this approach."

7C. Media and Minors: Effects of exposure to sexually explicit images on minors

●Dr. Henry Giarretto, founder and executive director of The Child Sexual Abuse Treatment Program in Santa Clara, California, the oldest such program and model for others around the country, said:

"Our program has not been designed to include collection of data on the use of pornography because the literature and our own clinical experience showed no link between the commission of child sexual abuse and sexually explicit material. While it has been clinically noted that some perpetrators read and/or view sexually explicit material, many others express their feeling that pornography is immoral. In contrast to common belief, a great number of men who turn to their children for sexual purposes are highly religious or morally rigid individuals who feel that this is 'less of a sin' than masturbation or seeking sexual liaisons in an outside affair." (statement from the Child Sexual Abuse Treatment Program, April 1991)

●The Surgeon General's report on pornography (1986) found little evidence that children, ages 10–17, view X-rated material.

●In questioning before the Ontario District Court in 1989, Donnerstein said:

"A.: The research presented to the Surgeon General of the United States was the most complete statement of what adolescents view.... the substantial majority of viewing really occurs in the PG-13 and R-rated form. There is very little evidence, very little evidence, in the surveys that children see anything X-rated whatsoever.

"Q.: By 'children,' what age group are you talking about?

"A.: Here we would be talking about those from age 10 through 17 or 18."

●In a longitudinal study measuring exposure to sexual material on TV at age 10 or 11 and sexual practice at age 16, J. Peterson, K. Moore and F.

Furstenburg found that exposure to sexual images had no effect on later sexual practice. ("Television Viewing and Early Initiation of Sexual Intercourse: Is There a Link," paper to the American Psychological Association, 1984)

●In 1988, Dr. Bradley Greenberg (chair of the Telecommunications Department, Michigan State University) et al. studied the effect on high schoolers of television programs that included prostitution, sexual intercourse (married and unmarried) and homosexuality. They found that the children's understanding of sexual terminology increased with viewing, but that there were *no* effects on the teens' beliefs or values regarding monogamy, prostitution, extramarital or premarital sex or homosexuality. (B. Greenberg, R. Linsangan, A. Soderman, C. Heeter, "Adolescents and Their Reactions to Television Sex," 1988, Report #5, Project CAST)

●A majority of studies show that of all available sources of information about sex, children and teenagers rely most on their peers. (Catherine Chilman, *Adolescent Sexuality in a Changing American Society*, 1983, New York, Wiley; J. Mancini and S. Mancini, *Journal of Sex Education and Therapy*, 1983, vol. 9, pp. 16–21)

Although one study shows that reliance on radio, television and school sex education programs is increasing (R. Fabes and J. Strouse, "Perceptions of Responsible and Irresponsible Models of Sexuality: A Correlational Study," *Journal of Sex Research*, 1987, vol. 23, pp. 70–84), a 1986 national poll found that teenagers rank the media as fourth as a source of information about sex, after friends, parents and schools. (Louis Harris and Associates, "American Teens Speak: Sex, Myth, TV, and Birth Control," 1986, New York, Planned Parenthood Federation of America)

●Testifying to the Ontario District Court in 1989, Donnerstein reported that should the media have negative effects on viewers, particularly minors, those effects are mitigated by parents and community values. He said:

"There are the parental values, their church values, what they learn about in school or what they learn from mom and dad. And, in fact, I think the most interesting thing about all the research is that it tends to indicate that for the other 99.99 percent, if we as parents only sit down with those children and talk about violence on television, and talk about objectification in films, we actually mitigate the effects."

7C. Media and Minors: Effects of exposure to violence in the media on minors

●Summing up a large body of research of television violence and children, Donnerstein told the Ontario District Court in 1989:

"Children who are already aggressive, for whatever reason... tend to have certain preferences for violent programming.... With a lot of other processes going on, their interactions with classmates, how they do in school, how their parents reinforce aggression or how their parents reinforce what they watch, you find a relationship ... not a causal relationship, but a relationship between that early exposure and those particular kids and later aggressive behavior."

●The one long-term study measuring effects of TV violence found that early viewing of violent programming accounted for 4–5 percent of adult violence (including run-ins with the law and domestic violence). (L. Eron and L. Huesmann et al., "Does Television Violence Cause Aggression?" *American Psychologist*, 1972, vol. 27, pp. 253–263)

●Suzanne Ageton's investigation of attitudes about women and real-life aggression among teenagers found that "involvement in a delinquent peer group appeared consistently as the most powerful factor," accounting for 76 percent of sexual aggression. Three other factors, including attitudes about women and violence, accounted for 19 percent altogether. (*Sexual Assault Among Adolescents*, 1983, Lexington, Massachusetts, Lexington Books, p. 119)

●Donnerstein stresses the importance of parental and community values, of sex education and of parents talking with their children about what they view and hear. He testified to the Ontario District Court:

"There are the parental values, their church values, what they learn about in school or what they learn from mom and dad. And, in fact, I think the most interesting thing about all the research is that it tends to indicate that for the other 99.99 percent, if we as parents only sit down with those children and talk about violence on television, and talk about objectification in films, we actually mitigate the effects."

8. POINTING THE FINGER

8A. Ted Bundy: Pornography made me do it

Ted Bundy, in an interview before his death, blamed pornography for leading him down a spiral of sexual violence that lead to serial murder.

In fact: social science researchers and those closest to Bundy doubt that sexually explicit imagery was the source of his crimes, and find Bundy's confession to be rationalization.

●Dr. Gene Abel (Emory University School of Medicine) said at the time of the Bundy execution:

"What we find is that sex offenders have rationalizations and justifications for their behavior. And Ted Bundy, like most of the sadists we've dealt with, had a lot of false beliefs or rationalizations to explain his behavior. What he said, in essence, was, 'It isn't my fault, these are pornographic things that I've seen.' And we just don't see that relationship."

●Dr. Emanuel Tanay, the psychiatrist who interviewed Bundy after his arrest in Florida, said:
"Pornography doesn't have the power to cause the severe deformity of personality that he had."

●Bundy's lawyer, James Coleman, said of Bundy's final interview: "It was vintage Bundy. It was Bundy the actor. He didn't know what made him kill people. No one did."

● Dr. Dorothy Lewis, professor of psychiatry at New York University and clinical professor at Yale University Child Study Center, conducted multiple interviews with Bundy and his family.

She discovered that, at age three, Bundy began evincing highly unusual behavior, like sticking butcher knives into his bed. At that time, Bundy and his mother were living with Bundy's grandfather, who according to family reports, was an extremely violent man. He beat and tortured animals, threw Bundy's aunt down a flight of stairs and generally terrorized the rest of the family. When Bundy was three, the family felt he and his mother should be moved out of the grandfather's household.

When Bundy was arrested in 1978, he was found not with violent pornography but with magazines advertising cheerleader camps. In his early interviews, he refers to popular sexual magazines as "normal, healthy sexual stimuli," and admits he was turned on by innocuous, not even explicitly sexual, fare. Only in the mid-eighties, when the court refused to declare Bundy insane and so remove the threat of the death penalty, did Bundy convert to born-again Christianity and begin collecting information attesting to the negative effects of pornography. By 1986, he was condemning popular soft-core magazines because they caused arousal for someone other than one's spouse.

In 1987, Bundy started quoting the research of Donnerstein and Linz on the change in attitudes about women found in lab settings after subjects were exposed to violent pornography. He failed to include the authors' insistence that in no study "has a measure of motivation such as 'likelihood to rape' ever changed as a result of exposure to pornography.... There is no reason to think that exposure to violent pornography is the cause of [a] predisposition [to rape]."

In his final interview, Bundy said, "The FBI's own study on serial homicide shows that the most common interest among serial killers is pornography."

In response, an FBI spokesperson said, "The FBI knows nothing about pornography." Its study contains two sentences on it. Dr. Ann Burgess, one of the authors of the FBI study, told the press that the FBI wasn't looking at pornography. "We never quantified it," she said. The Department of Justice rejected the FBI report for unacceptable methodology and statistics.

● The Kinsey Institute study of 1,356 men convicted of sex crimes found that they were less responsive to and less interested in pornography than prisoners convicted of nonsexual crimes or men in the general population. (Gebhard et al., *Sex Offenders*, 1965, New York, Harper & Row)

● Dr. Michael Goldstein et al. found that for rapists and child molesters, exposure to pornography during both adolescence and adulthood was less than for the general public. They also found that rapists were more likely to come from home environments in which education about sexuality was very limited and attitudes toward sex restrictive. (*Pornography and Sexual Deviance,* 1973, Los Angeles, University of California Press)

● In the *Harvard Civil Rights–Civil Liberties Law Review*, Barry Lynn (former legislative counsel, American Civil Liberties Union) wrote:
"Defendants accused of violent crimes against women have asserted that they were influenced by sources as diverse as the golden calf scene in Cecil B. DeMille's *The Ten Commandments* and an Anglican church service. For some defendants, of course, pornography has become a convenient excuse for their actions, an excuse more in tune with the times than blaming comic books and more plausible than blaming Twinkies [as convicted murderer of San Francisco Mayor George Moscone and Supervisor Harvey Milk claimed in his trial defense]....

"If a piece of feminist literature led even one man to respond with violence, should it too be regulated, under a theory that it caused him to feel threatened and triggered him to act out his aggression?

"Ironically, the more pathological an individual man is, the more difficult it will be to predict what will arouse him.... The fundamental argument is not about sexual imagery; it is whether we can afford to curtail speech because of its overt effect on a few people." (1986, vol. 21, p. 88)

8B. Victim testimony: Pornography made him do it

Victims of rape and sexual assault report that pornography played a role in the crimes against them.

In fact: Assigning blame for sex crimes to sexually explicit materials may relieve offenders of responsibility and serves the offender rather than the victim or society.

● Dr. Judith Becker and Ellen Levine, in their dissenting report to the Meese Commission, recognized that ascribing blame to sexual material is in the sex offender's interest. They wrote, "Information from the sex-offender population must be interpreted with care because it may be self-serving." (Becker and Levine, dissenting report, p. 11)

● Just as Ted Bundy tried to shift the blame for his crimes onto pornography, so, too, do survivors of sexual assault when they lay the blame on sexual imagery. They relieve their assailants of responsibility. Perhaps it is easier for a woman raped by someone she knows to blame an outside force for his violence rather than charge her assailant directly. It was also easier for Dan White to blame his assassination of San Francisco Mayor Moscone and Supervisor Harvey Milk on his consumption of Hostess Twinkies.

Ironically, survivors of sexual assault who blame sexually explicit material for the violence done them blame women for those crimes. Before the feminism of the 1970s, men got away with the "tight sweater" excuse. A skirt too short, a neckline too low made rape the woman's fault. According to blame-the-pornography logic, it's still the woman's fault—if not the woman in the sweater, then the image of the woman in the magazine. If not the woman in the room, then the image of the woman on the page, calendar or wall.

Attorney's Nan Hunter and Sylvia Law wrote in the Feminist Anti-Censorship Taskforce brief to the U.S. Court of Appeals, "Individuals who commit acts of violence must be held legally and morally accountable. The law should not displace responsibility onto imagery." (In *American Booksellers Association et al.* v. *William Hudnut III et al.*)

• In 1988, Ronald St. John confessed that he fatally stabbed his daughter because God told him to. The same year, Harry Ossip stabbed his three-year-old son because he "was satanic and the devil's baby." Immediately prior to going after his son with an eight-inch serrated blade, Ossip spent weeks walking around with his Bible clasped to his chest and attending Jehovah's Witnesses meetings.

In 1987, a Fort Lauderdale, Florida, evangelist beat his two-year-old daughter to death by "chastening" her with a belt. He confessed that he was "training" her according to Biblical injunction. The New Bethany Baptist Church Home for Boys in Walterboro, South Carolina, was raided in 1984 for similar "training" that included beating the children with a plastic pipe and confining them to small, unlit cells. School administrators defended their policies by quoting Proverbs 22:15, "Foolishness is bound in the heart of the child, but the rod of correction shall drive it far from him." Hundreds of instances like these come to the attention of the courts and press each year. (see Annie Gaylor's *Betrayal of Trust: Clergy Abuse of Children*, Madison, Wisconsin, Committee to Protect Children from Abusive Clergy)

In 1989, Oliver Thomas, general counsel for the Baptist Joint Committee on Public Affairs told the Associated Press that over 100 claims of child abuse by church workers had been filed nationwide. Two years later, in June 1991, the Presbyterian Church reported in its new policy on sexual misconduct that "between 10 and 23 percent of clergy nationwide have engaged in sexualized behavior or sexual contact with parishioners, clients, employees, etc., within a professional relationship." In a church survey of 50 presbyteries, 60 cases of sexual misconduct were being investigated. Rev. James Andrews, the denomination's chief administrative officer, told *The New York Times*, "It is a Christianity-wide plague." (June 12, 1991)

In 1986, a Hackensack, New Jersey, minister was convicted of sexually abusing a blind woman in his care. In 1988, evangelist preacher Tony Leyva admitted to sexual congress with more than 100 boys over a 20-year period. Police estimate the real count may be as high as 800.

Father Bruce Ritter, a Meese Commission member and former director of the Covenant House home for runaway teens, was accused by several boys of taking sexual advantage of them during their stay at Covenant. He resigned as head of Covenant House and was then investigated for fiscal improprieties by New York city authorities.

According to pornography-made-me-do-it logic, laymen and clergy who blame their crimes on what they read—on the teachings of God or Jesus—should be taken at their word. Society should grant that the Meese Commission and citizens groups such as the American Family Association have a point: people do blindly mimic what they read or see. On Ted Bundy logic, the country has no alternative but to ban the Bible.

8C. Teen suicide: Rock made them do it

The parents of Ray Belknap and James Vance went to court to prove that their sons' suicides were caused by the rock group Judas Priest.

In fact: the boys grew up in unstable and abusive households and were abusers of drugs and alcohol. The court found that it was unlikely that rock lyrics caused their suicides.

• In the Judas Priest trial, other information about Vance and Belknap came to light. Ray Belknap was 18; his parents split up before he was born. His mother married four times and her last husband regularly beat Ray. He also threatened Ray's mother with a gun in front of the boy, according to the police. Ray had quit high school after two years and was a heavy user of hallucinogens and cocaine. But the rock lyrics made him do it.

James Vance, Ray's friend, was born when his mother was 17. She beat him when he was a child, and when he got older, he beat her in return. He also had a history of drugs and boasted of drinking two six-packs of beer a day. But the rock lyrics made him do it. (*The New York Times*, September 20, 1990)

The court decided against Ray's and James's parents, who were seeking monetary compensation for their sons' deaths. The court ruled that Judas Priest rock group could not be considered the cause of the suicides. (*The New York Times*, August 25, 1990)

9. COMMUNITY VALUES

9A. Polls and public referenda on sexually explicit material

In fact: Recent polls indicate that Americans wish to preserve their right to read, view and hear the materials of their choice and object to infringements of that right.

•In the last five years, legislation to ban sexually explicit material has been rejected by voters or state legislatures in Michigan (1991), Maine and Cambridge, Massachusetts.

•In 1990, Penn and Schoen Associates conducted a national poll regarding the sale and display of books and magazines and found:

—84 percent of those polled said Americans "should have the absolute right to buy all magazines and books judged to be legal."

—92 percent agree that the "decision should be up to the individual to decide reading material."

—80 percent opposed restricting access to legal periodicals.

—73 percent said it was more important to protect the right to purchase books and magazines than to make sure magazines and books that some groups object to are kept off the shelves.

—More than 75 percent preferred the right to purchase objectionable books and magazines over the interest of the community in removing such objectionable publications.

—60 percent said restricting access to one type of magazine (e.g., men's magazines) would lead to restrictions on other material.

—80 percent said it was "unhealthy" for the government to decide what they should read.

—More than two thirds said the government should not discourage stores from selling particular books and magazines.

—56 percent said it was "unhealthy" for organized groups to engage in protest activity.

—58 percent opposed "picketing by citizens groups to pressure stores to remove magazines."

—56 percent described such picketing as censorship.

• A 1990 poll by Research and Forecasts Inc. showed that 80 percent of Americans favor maintaining or increasing National Endowment for the Arts funding.

—93 percent agreed that "even if I find a particular piece of art objectionable, others have a right to view it."

—81 percent said that "Congress should not pass laws that interfere with our right to free expression." (*Los Angeles Times,* April 20, 1990; *Chicago Tribune,* April 22, 1990)

9B. Community values and sales of sexually explicit material

Though it is popular to believe that only unhealthy or troubled people view pornography, and certainly no women, the sales receipts indicate otherwise.

In fact: Sexually explicit materials are purchased, rented and viewed by a wide range of the American public across the country, including many women.

• Nineteen eighty-nine saw 395 million rentals of adult-video tapes, most of which were watched by two or more people. Nineteen eighty-eight saw 398 million adult video rentals. ("Charting the Adult Industry," *Adult Video News Buyer's Guide*, 1991) That's 800 million viewings in one year—not including adult-video sales, cable tv viewings, mail-order adult-video sales, adult-theater viewings or adult-video viewings in private clubs.

• Forty-seven percent of adult-video rentals in 1989 were by couples or women alone. ("Charting the Adult Industry," *Adult Video News Buyer's Guide,* 1991)

• Phone sex in 1987 was a $2.4 million business—up from $1 million four years earlier. (*Sexuality Today*, May 4, 1987)

• Jack Humphrey, manager of a chain of video outlets in Florida, reported in the *St. Petersburg Times* that sales and rentals of adult tapes are up 85 percent between 1988 and 1990. "The biggest increase is in the number of women who come in," he said. "Now about 50 percent of our customers are women."

• In 1990, *Video Insider* magazine reported that *Playboy Sexy Lingerie II* ranked sixth on national video sales lists. Rental and sales of adult tapes trailed only new releases and children's tapes in national popularity. In the Northeast and West Coast, adult tapes surpass children's tapes in popularity and comprise up to 20 percent of a store's rentals.